TECHNIQUES OF
PROPAGANDA
&PERSUASION

Senior Editor:
Paul Moliken

Editors:
Darlene Gilmore & Sally Wein

Writer:
Magedah E. Shabo

Reviewing Teachers:
Heather Dennul

Peter Glaser

Cover and Text Design:
Maria J. Mendoza

Layout and Production:
Jeremy Clark

PRESTWICK HOUSE, INC.
"Everything for the English Classroom!"

ISBN: 978-158049-874-6

TABLE OF CONTENTS

INTRODUCTION...4

PART I: TECHNIQUES

Chapter 1: Assertion 11

Chapter 2: Bandwagon 18

Chapter 3: Card Stacking 24

Chapter 4: Glittering Generalities 30

Chapter 5: False Dilemma...36

Chapter 6: The Lesser of Two Evils..41

Chapter 7: Name-Calling 46

Chapter 8: Pinpointing the Enemy 52

Chapter 9: Plain Folk 58

Chapter 10: Testimonials 62

Chapter 11: Transfer 69

PART II: APPLICATIONS

Chapter 12: Desires and Fears...77

Chapter 13: The Desire for Love and the Fear of Rejection....................78

Chapter 14: The Desire for Prosperity and the Fear of Powerlessness 82

Chapter 15: The Desire for Immortality and the Fear of Death..............88

Chapter 16: Positive Uses of Propaganda 93

Chapter 17: Evoking Sympathy and Inspiring Generosity.......................95

Chapter 18: Promoting Civic Responsibility...104

Chapter 19: Negative Uses of Propaganda..116

Chapter 20: Provoking Fear and Hostility..117

Chapter 21: Promoting Discrimination, Violence, and Property Violation 124

Chapter 22: Dehumanization and the Violation of Human Rights.........131

Chapter 23: Deification 139

CONCLUSION...144

Cumulative Exercises 148

INTRODUCTION

WHAT IS PROPAGANDA?

Have you ever had a dramatic change of heart or a strong emotional response after looking at something as simple as a billboard or a commercial? If so, you may have been looking at propaganda. It is everywhere you turn, from the newspaper to the Internet to your favorite sitcom. In fact, we are so inundated with propaganda that much of what we see and hear inevitably affects us, informing everything from the brand of shampoo we buy to our ideologies and worldviews.

In its defense, propaganda is not always harmful; in fact, in some situations it has been considered benign, or even positive. However, by its very nature, propaganda is always manipulative; it is intended to give someone else control over your thoughts and actions. For that reason, it is crucial to be able to identify propaganda when you see it.

Propaganda comes in many forms. However, with some careful study, you can recognize propaganda by its:

- persuasive function
- sizeable target audience
- representation of a specific group's agenda
- use of faulty reasoning and/or emotional appeals

In the following chapters, we will take a closer look at these criteria and paint a more detailed picture of the phenomenon we call "propaganda." We will also discuss some of the most popular techniques of propaganda and their most common uses—both constructive and harmful.

By the time you have finished reading this book, you should be an informed consumer of media, well equipped to detect and analyze most of the propaganda you encounter. More importantly, as you gain practice in discerning the motives, tactics, and logic behind the messages you are exposed to, you will be empowered to make more rational, conscious decisions about how you live your life.

RECOGNIZING PROPAGANDA

Not all persuasive messages that target large audiences qualify as propaganda. In fact, even when such messages promote a specific agenda, they are often based on perfectly legitimate, soundly reasoned arguments. In propaganda, by contrast, logic is replaced with faulty reasoning, emotional appeals, or a combination of the two.

However compelling it may seem at first glance, true propaganda does not stand up to scrutiny. For example, take the following poster:

This World War I poster claims that *you* can save this family by contributing to the Women's Apparel Association. It also claims that if you fail to donate, you are directly responsible for the deaths of these three individuals. However, even if we assume that your contribution to the Apparel Unit really would keep an entire family alive, and not merely clothe a few individuals, there is no way to know whom your donation is reaching. The particular family in the drawing may not even exist. Hence, it is probably impossible to fulfill the guilt-inspiring command, "Don't let them die." This poster is an example of propaganda that combines faulty logic with an emotional appeal.

In other cases, however, a propagandist may attempt to bypass reason altogether by exploiting emotions. By appealing to feelings, rather than logic, the propagandist can trigger automatic, instinctive responses and lead people to draw hasty and false conclusions. In a world saturated with propaganda, it is important to recognize that emotions can easily be manipulated. Feelings, therefore, should play a secondary role in most decision-making processes.

In the following image, we see an example of a strictly emotional appeal. There is no semblance of an argument; the image is simply meant to inspire fear.

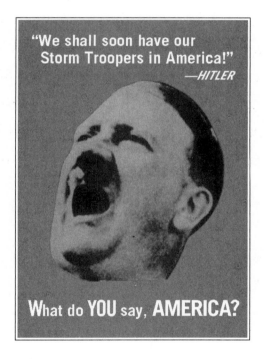

These examples of propaganda originated in the United States during the two World Wars. However, propaganda can still be found today, all over the world, and its very prevalence can easily lull us into a false sense of security. The same medium that convinces us to buy a certain brand of toothpaste one day may be used the next day to condone nuclear war. That is why it is important to stay alert for faulty reasoning and emotional appeals.

In the chapters that follow, we will explore some of the specific techniques propagandists use to circumvent logic, as we look at eleven of the most basic categories of propaganda. In the discussion of each form, you will find a number of examples, some historical, and others resembling messages you might see today. As you read about each form and look at the examples, try to recall where you may have seen such propaganda before, and consider the role propaganda might be playing in your daily life.

> Propaganda is a persuasive and widespread message designed to represent the interests of a particular group. However, what truly sets propaganda apart from other techniques of mass communication is that it attempts to bypass logic through faulty reasoning and emotional appeals.

DISCUSSION TOPICS

These questions are intended as starting points for class discussions; for most, there is no right or wrong answer. However, all responses should be defended in a way that demonstrates an understanding of the principles of propaganda that have been discussed in this chapter.

1. What are some potential sources of propaganda in the modern world?

2. In order to qualify as propaganda, a message must meet the following criteria:

- persuasive function
- sizeable target audience
- representation of a specific group's agenda
- use of faulty reasoning and/or emotional appeals

Describe an example of a message that would meet all but one of these criteria. Explain your answer.

3. Identify an example of propaganda you have recently been exposed to, and explain to the class why this message constitutes propaganda.

PART I: TECHNIQUES

CHAPTER 1: ASSERTION

The first, and simplest, form of propaganda is *assertion*. Despite being the most basic technique of propaganda, assertion is surprisingly effective. It consists of simply stating a debatable idea as a fact, with no qualification or explanation.

The Middle East will never be at peace.

A record number of hurricanes have been caused by global warming.

Assertion relies on the premise that people like to believe what they are told—that humans are, essentially, gullible, especially when the assertion made is something they want to believe.

Women are bad drivers.

Men never stop to ask for directions.

This technique is sometimes used in political and military propaganda, as in the following illustration from World War I.

However, assertions are perhaps even more visible in commercial advertising; the entire field is dedicated to making you believe a company's claims about its products.

Fulmer's Glue—making life better since 1926

Dogs that eat Nutri-Chow have more energy.

Think of how many advertisements include the following phrases, without any justification:

the best product available

the most popular brand

with a taste that will never let you down

When no explanation is offered, there is really no reason for a consumer to believe the advertiser's claims. After all, it is unlikely that any one product could objectively qualify as "the best," and almost every product will disappoint someone, at some time. However, all too often, consumers simply accept assertions, not recognizing that they are being influenced by a form of propaganda.

A common example of the assertion technique is the claim, made by myriad restaurants, that theirs is "the best chili in the world!" Often, a number of establishments in the same city will make the same claim. Of course, it can't be true for all of them. However, product advertisements are governed by a strange set of laws that allows businesses to claim titles like "the best" quite freely. This is peculiar logic, to be sure—and that is precisely why this kind of advertising qualifies as propaganda.

When we see simple assertions, we usually absorb their messages on some level, even if we are not conscious of their impact. Advertisers long ago learned one of the fundamental lessons of propaganda: once someone has absorbed a message, the battle is essentially won. Thus, assertion offers a quick and easy way to gain a foothold in people's minds.

This German World War II poster makes the assertion that "Europe's victory is your prosperity."

Consider an example from George Orwell's fictional study of propaganda and mind control, *1984*. In the novel, the following three slogans of "the Party" are emblazoned on the walls of the Ministry of Truth building:

WAR IS PEACE

FREEDOM IS SLAVERY

IGNORANCE IS STRENGTH

Propaganda that uses assertion does not always leave it at that, however. An assertion can also suggest a course of action, as in the following example.

Often, an assertion will also be supported by "facts" that are not necessarily true. By fabricating evidence that seems to verify the assertion, the propagandist reinforces the message. Rather than simply stating that a product is the best available, an advertiser might, instead, claim that "nine out of ten experts agree" that this product is the best.

The use of propaganda in advertising is not always dangerous. After all, manufacturers want people to buy their products, and if their toothpaste, cake mix, or other product does not live up to their claims, you have lost a few dollars and nothing more.

But consider the use of assertion to mislead people in a way that is potentially harmful or may not necessarily be in the public's best interest.

...the scientific evidence, taken as a whole, is insufficient to establish that other people's tobacco smoke is a cause of any disease. —Imperial Tobacco Group

As you assess statements like these, keep in mind the four qualifying characteristics of propaganda:

- persuasive function
- sizeable target audience
- representation of a specific group's agenda
- use of faulty reasoning and/or emotional appeals

The assertion from Imperial Tobacco meets the first three criteria. As for the fourth criterion, if there is any factual or logical basis for the assertion, it is not shared with the public.

A person who makes these types of simple assertions undermines the complexity of the issue at hand, substituting a simple declaration for a logical explanation. In general, unsupported assertions should not be given much credence. If someone wants to persuade you through a legitimate argument, he or she will present facts to support all claims.

In assertion, debatable ideas are stated as facts, with little or no explanation or justification.

DISCUSSION TOPICS

These questions are intended as starting points for class discussions; for most, there is no right or wrong answer. However, all responses should be defended in a way that demonstrates an understanding of the principles of propaganda that have been discussed in this chapter.

1. What makes a statement an example of assertion propaganda?

2. Describe several examples of assertions you have seen in politics and advertising. Do you think that these claims have affected your point of view? Explain your reaction.

3. Identify which of the following assertions qualify as propaganda, and explain your answer. Modify those that are not propaganda to make them fit the four criteria.

Parent to child: "If you eat your vegetables, you'll grow up to be big and strong."

Billboard: "Mario's Pizza, Next Exit."

Magazine Ad for Age-Defying Makeup: "True Beauty is Timeless."

Commercial: "According to a study by the National Heart Association, eating this cereal, as part of a balanced breakfast, may reduce the risk of heart disease."

Political commentator: "Richard Williams obviously doesn't have the experience it takes to be President of the United States."

4. Identify the audience and purpose for the following poster, and discuss whether this is an example of assertion propaganda.

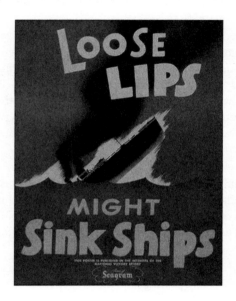

CHAPTER 2: BANDWAGON

As we have discussed, the assertion technique takes advantage of our desire to believe what we're told. The *bandwagon* technique, by contrast, exploits what is sometimes referred to as "the herding instinct." People like to belong to the majority group and dislike being left out. The bandwagon technique manipulates people by appealing to these instincts.

The term "bandwagon" has its origins in the 1800s, when politicians used wagons with music and entertainment to attract audiences. Once a sizeable crowd had gathered, the politician would speak. Other politicians, recognizing the popularity of certain bandwagons and hoping to take advantage of their success, would often try to get a seat on the bandwagon. In their haste to gain popularity, these politicians would often end up joining causes they did not believe in, just to be part of a winning team.

The phrase "jumping on the bandwagon" was used to describe this political phenomenon, and, eventually, the term was used outside the political realm. In modern usage, the term "bandwagon effect" refers to any situation in which people attempt to be part of a successful or popular endeavor merely for the sake of its popularity.

Five million members and growing!

Thousands of satisfied customers can't be wrong.

You may have experienced this persuasive approach in the form of peer pressure. If you have ever been told to do something simply because "everyone else is doing it," you were being encouraged to follow the logical fallacy of the bandwagon appeal. This technique can be very compelling. After all, why would "everyone" do something that was not worth doing? The problem with this reasoning, however, is that you do not know how other people made their decision; it may be that everyone is simply going along with what is popular.

This German poster reads "All the people say yes on April 10th!" The suggestion is that, since everyone else is supposedly voting "yes," you should too.

The bandwagon technique can be seen in a number of different scenarios. It might be used casually, on a topic that's not particularly controversial:

Everyone knows that the Grand Canyon is the most beautiful site in North America.

Or, it might be used to validate a moral claim:

More and more couples are living together without being married, so it must be all right.

Similarly, it might be used to promote a candidate or a product:

The Jackson campaign has the popularity it takes to win the election.

Choose the top-selling truck in its class.

The bandwagon technique is especially visible in product marketing. Advertisers will try to convince you that by failing to do what "everyone else" is doing or use the product "everyone else" is using, you are missing out.

Join the Digital Revolution.

In politics, the bandwagon appeal may be used to drum up support for a cause. Often, a military action will enjoy little public support until it appears that victory is likely. Once victory seems probable, people are quick to show that they support the war and have done so all along.

The reverse phenomenon can also be seen when a war seems to be a lost cause. As it becomes more and more apparent that victory is impossible, people withdraw their support. Both governments and activists will make use of the bandwagon technique in order to garner support for—or opposition to—a war.

In this example of bandwagon propaganda from World War I, sailors from Japan, France, the United States, Britain, Russia, and Italy are depicted as a happy band of brothers. The implication is that everyone is enlisting in the Navy, and those who don't should feel left out.

In the sciences, the bandwagon technique is often used as a way to gain mainstream acceptance of a given theory. Since the general public may struggle to understand the science behind complex issues, groups of scientists may instead use the bandwagon technique, combined with an appeal to authority, to gain popular acceptance of their ideas.

Most scientists believe global warming is a result of human activity.

Experts agree that obesity contributes to the development of cancer.

In such cases, it often makes sense to consider the majority opinion, but only if you have reason to believe that it is founded in logic. For example, scientific knowledge is built largely on majority opinion, but these opinions are generally founded on scrupulous testing and reviews. Even such reasonable majority opinions can be wrong, however, and they should always be subjected to scrutiny. After all, scientists once believed that the sun revolved around the earth and that smoking was a harmless pastime.

The bandwagon technique is sometimes used in defense of claims that are true. However, regardless of the truth of the claims, any argument that relies on the bandwagon effect is based on flawed logic. Truth should be conveyed using sound, logical arguments, not merely by appeals to popularity. For example, take the following statement:

Most people accept that gravity exists; therefore, I will also accept that gravity exists.

The conclusion, that gravity exists, is true. Nevertheless, the logic is flawed. The law of gravity is not subject to popular approval; it exists independent of human beliefs.

But that is not the only problem with buying into bandwagon propaganda. After all, how can you even know that the claim to popularity is true? As we already learned, the most basic technique of the propagandist is *assertion*—making an unjustified claim. Building on this method, propagandists may simply assert that something is popular, without any justification for this claim.

Look at the underlying logic of any argument, and judge that logic on its own merits, rather than depending on the decisions of the masses. After all, if one person can be wrong, so can a million—no matter what advertisers may tell you.

> **The bandwagon technique takes advantage of the human desire to be a part of the majority group or the winning team.**

DISCUSSION TOPICS

These questions are intended as starting points for class discussions; for most, there is no right or wrong answer. However, all responses should be defended in a way that demonstrates an understanding of the principles of propaganda that have been discussed in this chapter.

1. What makes the bandwagon technique appealing to most people?

2. Identify a decision you have made based primarily on popular opinion. Describe the situation, and explain whether following the majority made sense in that context.

3. Does the fact that numerous experts agree about a theory ever constitute logical grounds for accepting it? Explain your answer.

4. Identify the audience and purpose for the following poster, and discuss whether this is an example of bandwagon propaganda.

CHAPTER 3: CARD STACKING

Card stacking is a technique in which the propagandist gives an unfair advantage to one point of view, while weakening another. While arguments that use the card-stacking technique are usually honest in terms of the information shared, they may be misleading because they present information out of context or obscure important facts.

In this poster, the prospect of travel and adventure is strongly emphasized, both visually and verbally. The sacrifice required in exchange for this excitement, on the other hand, is obscured at the bottom of the page in the phrase, "Enlist to-day for 2-3 or 4 years."

Arguments that use card stacking are convincing because they often rely on sound reasoning and facts. The problem is that, in this technique, conflicting perspectives are unfairly downplayed; that is why card stacking is often referred to as the sin of omission.

A young doctor wants to practice a new surgical procedure on a patient. There are risks to the surgery that she does not disclose to the patient for fear that he will cancel the surgery.

Often, a propagandist will acknowledge alternative views, but in an oversimplified, dismissive way. This approach is often seen in debates that are orchestrated by someone with a vested interest in one side of the issue. Consider the following example:

A debate on global warming is organized by a group dedicated to limiting carbon emissions. The group invites two experts on different sides of the issue to speak. The expert invited to support carbon limits is a well known, eloquent speaker, with extensive scientific credentials. Conversely, the expert invited to represent the other side is a fringe scientist, known for a number of other exotic theories and for his loud, blustering demeanor.

In this situation, the impression of a fair debate is conveyed, but there is an underlying bias. The person who represents the opposition was chosen for his weaknesses: his unappealing demeanor, his unfavorable reputation, and his extremist views that are likely to alienate listeners.

In written or visual propaganda, this one-sided effect can be accomplished by stating the preferred view first or by making it more noticeable. Information that is not favorable to the propagandist's case may be printed in a smaller typeface or in some way visually obscured. Thus, the propagandist cannot be accused of outright dishonesty, even though he or she has unfairly represented the situation.

People signing a contract are always warned to "read the fine print." Often, the tiny, barely legible print, containing the least attractive terms, will appear at the bottom of the last page.

Card stacking is commonly used in advertisements promoting diet programs that use "before and after" pictures. In the "before" picture, the person is overweight, and in the "after" picture, he or she is thinner. In some cases, however, the weight loss itself might not appear particularly extreme, but the deck is stacked by manipulating other factors in the images. If you look at any of these ads, you will probably notice that in the "after" image, the lighting and background are usually more flattering. The person may have a trendier hairstyle and more flattering clothes and makeup in the second photograph. She may also be smiling and looking more cheerful than she had before using the product. While you may notice a change in weight, you are likely to also be affected by these other visual cues—which, of course, have nothing to do with the diet.

In the above example, in addition to revealing the woman's weight loss, the "after" photograph also reveals card-stacking efforts. In the second photo, the subject's hair is styled, and she is wearing makeup. The lighting is also more flattering in the "after" image, and the woman is wearing jewelry. Each of these factors contributes to the impression that the product being advertised can make a person more attractive.

Censorship is an extreme form of card stacking. Rather than minimizing the exposure of an opposing view or painting one side of an argument in a more favorable light, censorship removes all other sides completely. This is different from simply omitting different perspectives because, in censorship, the other perspectives are actively eliminated. An advertising agency may choose not to mention its products' shortcomings—this is card stacking via omission. A government, however, can eliminate the expression of opposing viewpoints by using the force of the state to punish any violators—this is card stacking via censorship.

When faced with possible instances of card stacking, ask yourself the following questions:

- Are opposing viewpoints represented fairly?
- Does one side seem to be presented more thoroughly than the other?
- Does it seem that important factors are being ignored?

If the answer to these questions is "yes," card stacking is probably taking place.

Card stacking is "the sin of omission"—the trivialization or exclusion of conflicting viewpoints.

DISCUSSION TOPICS

These questions are intended as starting points for class discussions; for most, there is no right or wrong answer. However, all responses should be defended in a way that demonstrates an understanding of the principles of propaganda that have been discussed in this chapter.

1. Why is it often difficult to distinguish card-stacking propaganda from legitimate arguments?

2. What clues can help you make the distinction between card-stacking propaganda and legitimate arguments?

3. Describe the different forms card stacking takes in print advertisements and television commercials. What kinds of products are often advertised with card-stacking propaganda?

4. Identify the audience and purpose for the following poster, and discuss whether this is an example of card-stacking propaganda.

CHAPTER 4:
GLITTERING GENERALITIES

Glittering generalities is a colorful term for the appealing, but vague words that often appear in propaganda. Rather than explaining the use of these words, the propagandist leaves them to stand alone as a defense of his or her position. Without context or specific definitions, they serve the sole purpose of evoking certain feelings in the audience. If everything proceeds according to plans, these feelings then translate into unquestioning approval of whatever the propagandist says.

In this World War I poster, billions of dollars are requested in the name of "Liberty." Here, "liberty" is a glittering generality—a pleasant term that has no specific meaning.

Glittering generalities are used in both advertising and politics. Everyone, from political candidates to elected leaders, makes use of the same vague phrases so frequently that they seem like a natural part of political discourse. In the modern age of ten-second sound bites, glittering generalities can make or break a candidate's campaign.

*I stand for **freedom**—for a **strong** nation, **unrivaled** in the world. My opponent believes we must compromise on these ideals, but I believe they are our **birthright**.*

The propagandist will intentionally use words with strong positive connotations and offer no real explanation.

This 1943 Nazi poster makes the vague and unjustified claim that "Adolf Hitler is victory!"

Popular glittering generalities include:

- freedom/liberty
- strength
- security
- prosperity
- choice
- equality
- change

Under the right circumstances, each of these words holds strong, positive connotations. For instance, the phrase "freedom of choice," while it may be vague, has been effectively attached to everything from social causes to fast-food restaurants.

This poster asserts that "Americans will always fight for liberty," without explaining what this pleasant-sounding phrase means.

Most advertising slogans use glittering generalities to convey something about the product being advertised. Since a slogan must be short and pithy, using powerful words has an obvious advantage. In some ad campaigns, the slogan may be elaborated on later, but, in many cases, the glittering generality will simply be left on its own.

*Orange Cola: made from **the best ingredients on Earth**.*

Spotting glittering generalities is simply a matter of looking for vague, positive words that are not explained. A reasonable argument, by contrast, will justify the words being used, explaining exactly what they mean in context.

Without context or specific definitions, glittering generalities serve only to evoke emotions.

DISCUSSION TOPICS

These questions are intended as starting points for class discussions; for most, there is no right or wrong answer. However, all responses should be defended in a way that demonstrates an understanding of the principles of propaganda that have been discussed in this chapter.

1. Glittering generalities are a common part of political campaigns. Compose a list of glittering generalities you have heard in campaign slogans, in debates, or in the news media.

2. Like politicians and journalists, advertisers often use glittering generalities to promote their products. Create a list of glittering generalities that are commonly used in advertising.

3. Under what conditions are words like "freedom" and "choice" not glittering generalities? Use each word in a sentence that does not qualify as a glittering generality.

4. Identify the audience and purpose for the following image, and discuss whether, in the context of this poster, Lincoln's words are being used as glittering generalities. If so, which words stand out as glittering generalities? If not, why not?

CHAPTER 5: FALSE DILEMMA

An extremely common tool of the propagandist is the *false dilemma*. This fallacy is known by many names, including "black-and-white thinking," "false dichotomy," and "false choice." Most commonly, it consists of reducing a complex argument to a small number of alternatives and concluding that only one option is appropriate. One product always works, and the other never works. One group intends to save the country, and the other is out to ruin it. In reality, however, there are usually many possibilities that go unmentioned.

This German poster from World War II presents the false dilemma that either you stop talking or you are supporting "the enemy." The caption reads, "Shame on you, chatterer! The enemy is listening. Silence is your duty!"

There are many ways of presenting a false dilemma, but the most common method is the "single cause" or "single trait" approach. The view or product the propagandist is promoting is depicted positively, and all competition or opposing views are depicted in a negative light. This technique is used most often in political and ethical discourse. One option is described as being good, and the other is made to seem bad, or even evil. In this way, you are essentially required to choose the "good" option, regardless of whether there is a logical argument for it.

You are either an ally or an enemy.

This sort of reduction denies the existence of any neutral ground; the false dilemma portrays all those who fail to do exactly what is desired as if they were in complete opposition to the cause at hand.

The message of this poster from World War II is that if you don't join a car-sharing club, you are directly supporting Hitler.

Advertising often makes use of the false-dilemma technique as well. For example, consider an advertisement that shows a husband and wife—the husband holding a small boy by the hand, while the wife carries an infant in her arms—standing in the rubble of their ransacked living room. While the logo of a security company appears in the lower right corner of the television screen, a strong, masculine voice comments, "The best way to show your love is to keep them safe." The implication is clear. This husband and father did not love his family enough to equip his home with that specific brand of security system.

If you are not using White Bright Detergent, your clothes are not clean.

If you support Israel, you cannot possibly be in favor of a Palestinian state.

You can subscribe to Politics Weekly, *or you can stay uninformed.*

The false dilemma reduces all choices to a simple matter of "either/or." Either you conserve gasoline, or you're helping Hitler. Either you purchase a security system, or you do not love your family. Either you use a specific brand of detergent, or you wear filthy clothes. Either you agree with us, or you are a fool—or maybe even a villain.

In the real world, of course, most issues are not so simple. There is a spectrum of gray between black and white, and part of being a rational person is learning to make difficult decisions in a world of infinite possibilities.

When presented with a false dilemma, you are essentially forced to choose the option that is labeled "good," regardless of whether there is a logical argument for it.

DISCUSSION TOPICS

These questions are intended as starting points for class discussions; for most, there is no right or wrong answer. However, all responses should be defended in a way that demonstrates an understanding of the principles of propaganda that have been discussed in this chapter.

1. List some examples of false-dilemma arguments you have heard in real life.

2. What are some of the clues that can help you distinguish a false dilemma from a legitimate presentation of facts?

3. Following the examples provided in this chapter, create a false-dilemma argument to fit each of the following scenarios. (Hint: False dilemmas often take the form of "either/or" assertions.)

encourage recycling

endorse a political candidate

support a tax increase

4. Identify the audience and purpose for the following poster, and discuss whether this is an example of false-dilemma propaganda.

CHAPTER 6: THE LESSER OF TWO EVILS

While most false dilemmas offer a "good" and a "bad" alternative, the *lesser-of-two-evils* technique is a specific type of false dilemma that offers two "bad" alternatives. This technique is often used when the propagandist is trying to convince people to adopt a perspective they will be hesitant to accept. In order to make the choice more appealing, an even worse alternative is presented as being the only other option. It is argued that an imperfect option is, at any rate, better than the horrendous alternative.

Don't want to drive a fuel-efficient automobile? Try living under a terrorist regime!

In nations such as the United States, which has a de facto two-party system, the lesser-of-two-evils argument is often used as a selling point for politicians. For example, a candidate who is unpopular within his or her party may suddenly appear more attractive when pitted against a member of the opposing party.

Williams may have lied under oath, but at least he never embezzled money from his campaign, like his opponent.

In political elections, this tactic is frequently used to dissuade people from voting for third-party candidates. The majority parties often encourage voters who dislike both major candidates to choose the one they consider the lesser of two evils, rather than voting for a third-party representative who is unlikely to win. In the 2000 US presidential election, for example, the Democratic Party used this approach with its "Nader = Bush" bumper sticker. The message was that a vote for the liberal Green Party candidate, Ralph Nader, would be the equivalent of a vote for the conservative Republican, George W. Bush. Democrats presumed that even though many Nader supporters disliked Democrat Al Gore, they would still prefer Gore to Bush. In effect, the Democrats were portraying their candidate as the lesser of two evils.

Likewise, when governments ask for sacrifices from their people, it is often done using a lesser-of-two-evils approach. When the authorities know that the sacrifices they are asking for will not be received well, they preempt dissent by pointing out that the alternative would be far worse. Neither choice is a good one, but, given only these two options, the citizens must choose whichever they consider the lesser evil.

The lesser-of-two-evils technique is most effective when one of the alternatives is truly awful, as in the above example, which pits frugality against fascism. The propagandist aims to make people select an option they probably would not have chosen under different circumstances.

In many cases, the lesser of two evils approach is used to unite opposing factions. A common enemy or threat can often make other areas of disagreement seem trivial.

Hunters, environmentalists, animal-rights activists, and the medical community all agree that the threat to human life posed by the avian flu pandemic is so severe that the only possible solution is to destroy all species of birdlife on the planet.

If these two horrible choices were the only ones available, most people would probably unite to protect humanity.

While there are many flaws in the lesser-of-two-evils approach, the main problem is that, like the false dilemma, it usually ignores many alternative possibilities. Often, adopting a lesser-of-two-evils stance discourages innovative thinking by needlessly reducing the possible options.

It is always best to be suspicious of any message that purports to show you the only two (or three, or four) options available. Be especially wary if none of the options is desirable, but one is promoted as being merely better than the alternatives. When you're faced with such a choice, consider each option on its own merits, and keep in mind that there are probably other, undisclosed alternatives.

By using the lesser-of-two-evils technique, the propagandist would like to make you choose the better of two poor options, without considering other possibilities.

DISCUSSION TOPICS

These questions are intended as starting points for class discussions; for most, there is no right or wrong answer. However, all responses should be defended in a way that demonstrates an understanding of the principles of propaganda that have been discussed in this chapter.

1. How is the lesser-of-two-evils technique similar to the false-dilemma approach? What sets these techniques apart from one another?

2. What are the keys to identifying the lesser-of-two-evils fallacy?

3. The lesser-of-two-evils fallacy is often used to defend the status quo, as exemplified in the familiar idiom, "better the devil you know than the devil you don't know." Generate a list of real-life scenarios in which this technique of propaganda is used to preserve the status quo.

4. Create a caption to go with this image that would make this an example of lesser-of-two-evils propaganda.

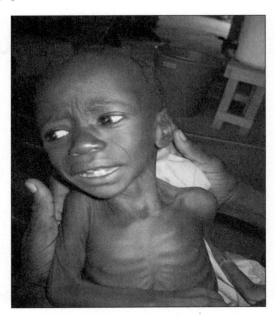

CHAPTER 7: NAME-CALLING

Pig!

Pinko!

Egghead!

Redneck!

Consider the words above, each used as a derogatory term for a certain type of person. Do any of the words evoke an emotional response? If you consider yourself a member of one of the groups attacked by these words—perhaps you are a good student and you consider the term "egghead" an insult—seeing the word may make you angry. It may even make you so angry that you are moved to retaliate and call the attacker a name in response. That is exactly what the propagandist wants.

Or, perhaps, you consider yourself a victim of sorts; for instance, you just received another speeding ticket and fail to understand the value of the police force. You may, in this situation, take pleasure in learning that someone else sees things from your perspective. You may want to meet that like-minded person, join forces, and strike out at your perceived opponent. At this point, calling names has helped the propagandist achieve his or her goal.

Name-calling is the use of negative words to disparage an enemy or an opposing view. Insulting words are used in place of logical arguments, appealing to emotions, rather than reason. In many ways, name-calling is the opposite of the glittering-generalities technique, which uses positive words in a similar way.

*He's one of the **looniest commies** on the left.*

Name-calling can take a number of different forms, depending on the circumstances, but they all follow the same general pattern. Rather than making a legitimate argument, the propagandist attacks the opposition on a personal level, often appealing to the audience's preconceptions and prejudices. Name-calling takes advantage of one of the darker sides of human nature: our propensity to classify competitors, or those we simply don't understand, as somehow inferior.

*John is just your average **right-wing gun nut**.*

The simplest form of name-calling is directly attacking a person or an idea. Direct name-calling is usually used if the target audience is already leaning in favor of the propagandist. For example, if a politician wanted to further discredit an already unpopular opponent, he or she might say:

*Clearly, my opponent's **anarchist** suggestions will not help to solve the current crisis.*

Such direct attacks are less effective if the target audience is sympathetic to the opponent, as the listeners will be more likely to see the name-calling for what it really is. It may even strengthen their support for the attacked idea or person. Remember, the propagandist's goal is to convince you to believe something or act in a certain way, so he or she will be well aware of which technique will work best with which audience.

In indirect name-calling, the propagandist takes a more subtle approach, perhaps making sarcastic or tongue-in-cheek remarks about an opponent. Rather than directly calling the opponent a derogatory name, the propagandist may, instead, make the same negative suggestions in a more jovial, less confrontational manner. This is much more effective when the target audience is somewhat sympathetic to the opponent.

*Although we all have a great deal of respect for Senator Parker, I'm not certain we need to accept his views on marriage without careful scrutiny. After all, he is a **confirmed bachelor**.*

In this instance, rather than openly attacking his or her opponent, the propagandist couches critical remarks with polite language and a claim of "respect." Nevertheless, calling the man a "confirmed bachelor" to invalidate his views on marriage is an example of a subtle approach to name-calling.

Among the most common venues for name-calling are political cartoons and political satire. In fact, two of the most famous political symbols in the United States had their origins in name-calling cartoons. In the 1828 presidential campaign, opponents of the Democratic-Republican Party candidate, Andrew Jackson, called him a "jackass." Jackson decided to embrace this comment, intended as an insult, and use the donkey as a symbol for strength and a strong will. From there, the strong-willed jackass eventually came to be associated with the Democratic Party in general, especially after political cartoonist Thomas Nast used the image in newspaper cartoons in the late nineteenth century.

"A LIVE JACKASS KICKING A DEAD LION."

And such a Lion! and such a Jackass!

Similarly, Nast popularized the symbol of the Republican elephant. In a cartoon that appeared in Harper's Weekly, in 1874, Nast drew a donkey (representing the Democratic Party) clothed in a lion's skin, scaring away all the animals in the jungle. One of those animals, the elephant, was labeled "The Republican Vote."

While Nast's intention was probably to suggest that Republicans were slow, plodding, and not open to innovation or change, the Republican Party quickly adopted the elephant as a symbol of strength and dignity.

Any time a label—especially a derogatory label—is attached to a person in order to discredit that person's argument, name-calling is being employed. It is always best to disregard such insulting language and look, instead, at a person or issue based on actual merits and flaws. Find out who stands to gain through the name-calling, and you'll be less likely to be manipulated by this form of propaganda.

> **While name-calling is frequently crude and obvious, it can be used very effectively against an unpopular target.**

DISCUSSION TOPICS

These questions are intended as starting points for class discussions; for most, there is no right or wrong answer. However, all responses should be defended in a way that demonstrates an understanding of the principles of propaganda that have been discussed in this chapter.

1. What are some examples of name-calling you have seen in advertising, politics, or popular culture?

2. In indirect name-calling, words that are not necessarily negative, in and of themselves, are used to subtly disparage an opponent. List some examples of words that can be used in this way, and describe a possible context in which they would be considered name-calling.

3. What makes name-calling a logical fallacy?

4. Identify the audience and purpose for the following poster, and discuss whether this is an example of name-calling propaganda.

Note: President Theodore Roosevelt coined the term "muckrakers" to describe journalists and politicians who were known for exposing social injustices.

CHAPTER 8: PINPOINTING THE ENEMY

Propagandists often oversimplify complex problems by pointing out a single cause or a single enemy who can be blamed. For everything from unemployment to natural disasters, *pinpointing the enemy* can help the propagandist achieve his or her agenda.

*The first thing we do, let's kill **all the lawyers*** —Henry VI, Part II: IV, ii

Problems rarely stem from a single cause, but propagandists often benefit from oversimplifying situations. People generally like clear-cut explanations, and politicians take advantage of this fact by pointing to a single enemy and placing all the blame at his or her feet.

This World War II poster identifies "the enemy" of the United States, giving a human face to the threat of fascism.

When the enemy in question is blamed for problems that are actually someone else's fault, this is a particular category of pinpointing the enemy known as *scapegoating.* Blaming a scapegoat alleviates the guilt of those who are truly at fault, while providing a convenient explanation for the problem at hand.

This 1854 painting by William Holman Hunt, "The Scapegoat," illustrates the origins of the term—the ancient Hebrew tradition of driving a goat into the wilderness on Yom Kippur to carry away the people's sins.

Pinpointing the enemy works particularly well when the targeted group is already thought of as "the other." An example of this phenomenon is the Nazi portrayal of the Jewish people as the source of economic problems in Germany. People who are easy to recognize by appearance or culture make perfect scapegoats; if they are easy to identify, they are easy to blame.

However, cruel dictators are not the only propagandists who make use of this technique. For example, activists often raise public awareness of their causes by pinpointing enemies.

*As long ago as 1987, a train system was developed. The train's motion is based on magnetic levitation, and it causes only minimal pollution. Versions of this train are already commonplace in several countries, but **the big American Oil Companies** have stifled all talk of bringing the trains here.*

Listening to the full story, in all its detail, can be overwhelming, leading people to become apathetic. Effective propaganda, therefore, will often define a complicated issue as having a single cause—and, often, a single enemy.

*Uncontrolled fishing by **greedy commercial fishers** has reduced the numbers of some fish to one-tenth of their original population.*

When presented in their entirety, our obstacles may seem insurmountable. Often, all we really want to know is, "Who's to blame?" And the propagandist is only too willing to tell us. A few "enemies" are pinpointed, and these are then targeted mercilessly.

McDougal's Burgers *are responsible for the obesity epidemic in America.*

Frequently, a single company will also be targeted, while others that may have similar or even worse practices go untouched. Companies such as Wal-Mart and Starbucks have served as scapegoats for many economic problems over the years. Generalized dislike for these huge companies has become so widespread that environmentalists and labor activists can use it to rally people behind other, often barely related, causes, such as a desire for unionization or discrimination against women.

Megamart *is responsible for the destruction of small businesses throughout the country.*

Most issues that confront us are complex, from the environment to the economy to international relations. Nevertheless, people are often eager to accept a simple answer to a complicated question. Remember that the propagandist's message is always based on faulty logic. Arguments that pinpoint a single enemy are usually fallacious because, even if "the enemy" is part of the problem, it's probably not the sole cause. The problem is being oversimplified.

By definition, propaganda must serve the interests of a particular person or group. So, who would benefit from pinning blame on a scapegoat? Certainly, a person with power might use this technique to defame a personal enemy or divert attention from his or her own wrongdoings. Likewise, a leader may use this technique, among others, to unite diverse factions against a common enemy; what better way is there to unite rival groups than to pit them against a third party?

Pinpointing the enemy plays on our desire to assign blame, making overwhelming problems seem quite simple and easy to solve.

By pinpointing an enemy, a propagandist assigns a single cause to a multifaceted problem.

DISCUSSION TOPICS

These questions are intended as starting points for class discussions; for most, there is no right or wrong answer. However, all responses should be defended in a way that demonstrates an understanding of the principles of propaganda that have been discussed in this chapter.

1. How is pinpointing the enemy similar to name-calling? How are the two techniques different?

2. Identify an instance of pinpointing the enemy that you have witnessed in the media. What companies, groups, or individuals have been blamed for many of the world's problems?

3. How is pinpointing the enemy related to "scapegoating," and the ancient Hebrew practice of driving a goat into the wilderness to take away the people's sins?

4. Identify the audience and purpose for the following poster, and discuss whether this is an example of pinpointing-the-enemy propaganda.

Note: The term "Hun" was used to refer to the Germans during World War I.

CHAPTER 9: PLAIN FOLK

People tend to distrust outsiders, and plain-folk propaganda can be used to take advantage of this common prejudice. The aim of this approach is to make an individual seem like an ordinary citizen, worthy of the public's confidence.

In this poster from George McGovern's 1972 presidential campaign, the senator's face blends in among the smiles of "plain folk" of various ages, ethnicities, and professions.

The plain-folk approach can perhaps be seen most strikingly in political candidates. Politicians often strive to be seen as more normal than their opponents. They might do this by dressing like the average citizen, using colloquial expressions, dropping the "g" from "-ing" verbs, or cultivating a working-class persona. Often, such behaviors are merely part of a politician's strategy and do not reflect who he or she really is.

Former President Bill Clinton ate at McDonald's, played the saxophone on a late-night talk show, and admitted to enjoying spy novels.

Former President Ronald Reagan was often photographed chopping wood.

Former President James Carter insisted on being sworn into office as "Jimmy."

In recent years, perennial Washington office-holders have been blamed for many of the problems in the United States government. This trend has made it more important than ever for political candidates to be seen as "plain folk." To emphasize their own connections to the average citizen, candidates will often attack the credibility of their opponents by labeling them "Washington insiders" or "elitists."

The plain-folk technique can be effective even in international situations. For example, with this approach, foreign "enemy" soldiers can be depicted as normal, everyday people who have families, hopes, and dreams. This strategy may undermine the opposition's will to fight; after all, fellow fathers, mothers, and children are more difficult to kill than are nameless, faceless enemies.

Plain-folk propaganda portrays its subject as humble and relatable. Common techniques include:

- the use of colloquial phrases or intentional mistakes in pronunciation that give the propagandist's speech a rougher, more working-class feel
- expressions of extreme sentimentality, such as fighting back tears when talking about a tragedy
- using words such as "home," "children," or "dinner table" that evoke the idea of the average family
- an appearance of shyness, or a seeming reluctance to take the spotlight or a position of leadership

Although it is generally effective, the plain-folk technique sometimes backfires. Propagandists using this approach may seem insincere if they are not careful. For example, President George Herbert Walker Bush took on an "average Joe" persona by expressing his penchant for fishing and his lifelong aversion to broccoli. This plain-folk approach worked fairly well until a reporter asked him the price of a gallon of milk. Bush's inability to come up with a realistic estimate revealed how distant his lifestyle was from that of most working Americans and damaged his efforts at seeming like an ordinary person.

Plain-folk propaganda portrays and individual as an "average Joe" to gain the public's trust.

DISCUSSION TOPICS

These questions are intended as starting points for class discussions; for most, there is no right or wrong answer. However, all responses should be defended in a way that demonstrates an understanding of the principles of propaganda that have been discussed in this chapter.

1. What are some examples of plain-folk propaganda that you have seen in advertising? What product lines have used this technique, and how?

2. What kinds of advertisements and/or political campaigns would not benefit from using the plain folk approach? Under what circumstances would this technique be counterproductive?

3. Consider the following quote:

> I grew up on a farm in rural Mississippi, so I know the meaning of struggle. I learned the value of hard work and determination at an early age, and it's a lesson I won't soon forget.

Describe a situation in which this quote would constitute plain folk propaganda. Then, describe a scenario in which it would not.

CHAPTER 10: TESTIMONIALS

Testimonials are a form of propaganda that is familiar to nearly all of us. Almost everything that is advertised comes with some sort of testimonial, from music, to hair gel, to politicians. Testimonials take advantage of the fact that there are certain people we tend to trust—even if that trust is based on mere recognition rather than true credibility. The propagandist can, therefore, use testimonials to convince us of something, regardless of whether there is any logical reason for us to be convinced.

An Olympic gold medal winner claims that she eats Golden Flakes every morning.

Most testimonials—both in politics and in advertising—are made by famous people. You may read that an actor you admire supports a certain political candidate. You may see a singer you like using a certain cell phone. You may watch a commercial in which a popular athlete advises you to buy a certain pair of shoes. Every day, we are flooded with endorsements from famous people, encouraging us to buy, use, and vote for the same things they do.

Movie stars and models are often paid to give testimonials in which they attribute their beauty and success to a given product.

The goal of the propagandist who uses testimonials, of course, is that your feelings toward the famous person will transfer to the product or cause he or she is endorsing. Thus, the propagandist hopes to make you commit a serious error of judgment, placing trust in a person who has not proved his or her credibility and who has probably been paid for the endorsement.

For instance, a person may love Sean Penn's movies and even agree with some of his political views, but that does not qualify him to pick out the ideal presidential candidate. A basketball player might be able to dunk the ball with ease, but that doesn't mean he has extraordinary knowledge about batteries—the brand he uses probably has nothing to do with his success.

In this World War II poster, the familiar face of heavyweight champion boxer Joe Louis encourages Americans to contribute to the war effort.

To avoid being taken in by this form of manipulation, it is best to first examine our reasons for admiring a given celebrity, and then decide whether he or she is qualified to make a decision on your behalf.

A famous 1980s television commercial featured an actor who played a doctor on a long-running television show. In the commercial, wearing a white lab coat and stethoscope, he would say to the audience, "I'm not really a doctor, but I play one on TV." He would then extol the benefits of a certain over-the-counter medication.

In this case, the advertiser's purpose is to capitalize on the audience's mental association between the actor and the medical profession. The propagandist's hope is that you will trust the "doctor" and use the advertised medication.

Of course, in daily life, there are many testimonials that should be heeded. For example, you should be able to trust your accountant to give you good advice about your taxes, and it should be safe to believe your neighbor's testimony about the camera she bought last year. Most likely, neither of these people has anything to gain by misleading you.

Remember, in order to constitute propaganda, a testimonial must have the following traits:

- persuasive function
- sizeable target audience
- representation of a specific group's agenda
- use of faulty reasoning and/or emotional appeals

Most often, the key to recognizing testimonial-based propaganda is to investigate the possible ulterior motives of those giving the testimonial. As a rule, the celebrity or "expert" witness will be compensated for his or her testimony. Hence, while you may be able to trust your own doctor, there may be doctors who recommend certain medications simply because they are paid by the pharmaceutical company. In fact, if a doctor appears in a television or print ad or in a late-night "infomercial," you can be certain that he or she is receiving some form of compensation for the testimonial.

Many have caught on to this technique and are put off by paid celebrity or "expert" endorsements. As a result, many advertisers and political campaign managers take a different approach—the "plain-folk testimonial." In this type of endorsement, the testimony comes not from a famous actor, athlete, or scientist, who is obviously being compensated, but from an average-looking student, homemaker, or taxi driver. Campaign ads often feature endorsements from ordinary men and women working in their gardens, grocery shopping, or jogging in the park, who support their particular candidate so strongly that they are willing to pause in their busy routines and tell you why.

A commercial for a particular brand of mattresses features not only its famous spokesperson, but also a number of "real people" who claim to sleep much better since purchasing this bed.

The promoters of a popular over-the-counter weight loss product feature "before and after" photographs of ordinary people, in addition to a few famous spokespeople who have successfully lost weight using this product.

Testimonial propaganda is also found frequently in politics. Military actions are often supported by "think tanks" and institutions that most of us have never heard of—yet, somehow, their words make us more confident. Politicians line up to support a bill and ask us to take their word for it, rather than having us investigate the issue ourselves. Likewise, doctors, sports figures, people in the entertainment business, religious leaders, and other famous people are frequently quoted as supporting a wide range of medications, products, and services, some of which are good for you and some of which are not.

Of course, just as not every testimonial is propaganda, not every expert opinion is a testimonial. Take movie and book reviews, for example. Legitimate, professional reviewers have some expertise in the field and are never paid by the industry they review. That is the only way the reviewer can remain free to give the movie, book, or product the rating he or she truly thinks it deserves.

We are surrounded by experts—many self-proclaimed—all with their own opinions and recommendations. However, testimonials are dangerous only when you are being asked to trust someone who has a vested interest in a certain outcome, or someone who has no expertise in the field.

> **The goal of the propagandist is that your trust in the celebrity, expert, or "plain folks" who give the testimonial will carry over to the product or cause at hand.**

DISCUSSION TOPICS

These questions are intended as starting points for class discussions; for most, there is no right or wrong answer. However, all responses should be defended in a way that demonstrates an understanding of the principles of propaganda that have been discussed in this chapter.

1. What qualifies a person to give a trustworthy, legitimate testimonial?

2. What are some of the warning signs that cast suspicion on a testimonial?

3. Imagine that you are an advertiser, attempting to market a product. How would you go about using the testimonial technique in a way that appears trustworthy?

4. Identify the audience and purpose for the following poster, and discuss whether this is an example of testimonial-based propaganda.

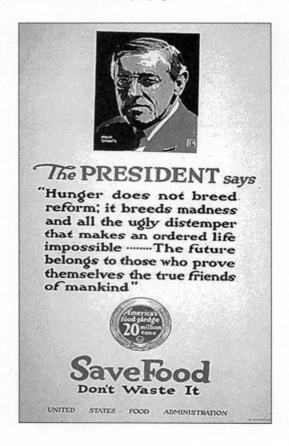

CHAPTER 11: TRANSFER

The final technique we will cover is the subtle but dangerous method known as transfer. Also known as "association" and "false connection," transfer is closely related to the testimonial technique. In this method, the propagandist encourages the transfer of feelings and associations from one idea, symbol, or person to another.

Baseball, hot dogs, and apple pie; they go together in the good ole' USA.

An automobile manufacturer that wants to be known as environmentally friendly films its car riding through a pristine forest. Friendly forest animals eagerly look on—and do not run away—as the car passes.

A candidate for office addresses allegations of wrongdoing in front of a house of worship while wearing a religious symbol on his lapel pin.

Some symbols are fairly straightforward. The Democratic Donkey and the Republican Elephant represent the actions and ideologies of their respective parties. The symbol of the skull and crossbones warns the viewer of danger or calls to mind the violent pillaging of a pirate raid. A dove signals peace. Some symbols, however, will mean one thing to one person and quite the opposite to another person. The propagandist's challenge is to use symbols that are appropriate to his or her audience.

For example, the American flag is meant to evoke positive feelings and ideas; it stands for freedom, courage, and equality. At its most basic, it is meant to represent something good, and Americans, in general, are expected to react positively to this image. However, some may view this symbol in quite a different light. In a nation at war with the United States, for example, citizens might attach fear or resentment to the stars and stripes.

In this image, directed at the American public, President Franklin Delano Roosevelt attempts to transfer the trust and respect associated with the American flag to himself and his administration.

The history of the swastika illustrates just how controversial and ambiguous a symbol can be. Although it is best known in the West as the symbol of Hitler's Nazi party, the swastika originated in the region of modern-day India as a symbol of well-being and good fortune. Ironically, the image of the swastika has gone from a pleasant sign of prosperity to a hated symbol of totalitarianism, racism, and genocide. In fact, in much of the world, this symbol has become synonymous with evil.

In this image, the once benign swastika represents evil itself. The feelings of fear and anger associated with the Nazi Party are evoked by this simple symbol.

So far, we have discussed the American flag and the swastika. However, there are many different kinds of symbols. For example, a symbol often seen in advertising is the white lab coat, commonly associated with knowledge and science.

Advertisers or public relations directors who are trying to gain your trust may have their spokesperson wear a white lab coat. The spokesperson need not be a scientist, but the positive associations we have with science will likely transfer and bolster our opinion of the product.

Transfer may also be used in ways that are more obvious. The image of a Ku Klux Klan member in a white, peak-hooded robe, blazing torch in hand, has come to instill a sense of fear and disgust in most Americans. A campaign trying to undermine a particular politician might, therefore, run a negative ad campaign in which images of KKK gatherings are superimposed over images of his inaugural ceremony. This is a blatant transfer of negative emotions, but such tactics can, nonetheless, be quite effective.

In this World War II poster, the symbols for Japan (left) and Germany (right) appear on clawed hands, grasping at a mother and child. The fear and outrage inspired by these hands is meant to transfer a sense of outrage against these enemy nations.

In addition to transferring a specific emotion, the technique of transfer can also be used to shift blame from one group to another—a form of scapegoating—or to shift approval from one group to another—a form of bandwagoning. Many politicians have their pictures taken in the presence of successful people with whom they want to be associated, or use body language to distance themselves from "fallen" people or causes.

There is nothing wrong, of course, with the president of the United States delivering a speech while sitting in the Oval Office, an American flag to his or her right. Likewise, it is appropriate for a state's district attorney to hold a press conference on the steps of the state courthouse. The presence of symbols becomes propaganda only when the symbols are intended to send an unspoken message that appeals to the emotions.

In the technique known as "transfer," propagandists try to circumvent logic by encouraging their audiences to transfer emotions and associations from one thing to another.

DISCUSSION TOPICS

These questions are intended as starting points for class discussions; for most, there is no right or wrong answer. However, all responses should be defended in a way that demonstrates an understanding of the principles of propaganda that have been discussed in this chapter.

1. What is a symbol that most people in your community would view as positive, and what specific associations would this symbol transfer?

2. What is a symbol that would evoke a negative response from your community? What negative associations are attached to this symbol?

3. Describe an instance of transfer that you have witnessed in advertising, politics, or some other public arena, and explain to the class why this qualifies as transfer.

4. Identify the audience and purpose for the following poster, and discuss whether this is an example of transfer propaganda.

PART II: APPLICATIONS

CHAPTER 12: DESIRES AND FEARS

Now that we have looked at some of the most common forms propaganda takes, we are ready to discuss how it is used. In all of its various forms, propaganda is fundamentally geared toward one specific goal: changing how you act. And the best way to accomplish this end is to affect the way you think and feel. The propagandist ultimately wants you to do something: buy a product, fight a war, vote for a candidate, or use a service. The most effective propagandists know your weaknesses, know what emotions and thoughts affect you, and know how to get you to do what they want.

We've already discussed the fact that emotions are a powerful manipulative tool. Now, we'll take a look at the various ways propagandists use our feelings against us to suit their own ends. Most actions are motivated by desires and fears, and the skilled propagandist can use either feeling against you, in the appropriate circumstances.

Often, the difference between fear and desire is simply a matter of perspective. Many fears and desires are two sides of the same coin. Propagandists must decide which side to present, calculating whether fear or desire will be a better manipulative tool in a given context. For example, they may have to decide whether to emphasize:

- the desire for popularity or the fear of being left out
- the desire for affluence or the fear of poverty
- the desire for health or the fear of disease

Your job, as an informed consumer of propaganda, is to recognize manipulative tactics when you see them, so that you can make sound decisions, regardless of fear or desire. In the following chapters, we'll go over the most common fears and desires propagandists appeal to. Then, we'll show you some of the ways propagandists can put your emotions to work for various causes—both good and evil.

By controlling your emotions, the propagandist ultimately gains control over your behavior.

CHAPTER 13: THE DESIRE FOR LOVE AND THE FEAR OF REJECTION

People are social creatures. Most of us are highly dependent on the acceptance and love of our peers. We want other people to like and respect us. We want to feel as if we're part of a family or tribe. We want others to love us and show us affection, and we fear being rejected and unloved. Propagandists know we have these needs and use them to advance specific agendas.

THE DESIRE FOR LOVE

Advertisers often use the desire for love to sell their products. Often, this is done simply by associating a product with images of people displaying mutual affection. The problem with these kinds of advertisements is that they encourage you to base your decisions on feelings alone. In the adjacent ad, for example, we are encouraged to buy a certain product based on the promise of romance. However, the manufacturer provides no evidence that this product will actually achieve the desired results, nor is there any mention of other benefits or drawbacks.

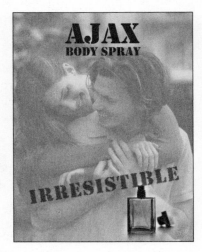

Good advertising propaganda will take this tactic a step further, creating a cult of popularity around a product or service. The product is portrayed as a status symbol, and those who buy it are encouraged to see themselves as members of an elite group. This kind of advertising is particularly effective in the marketing of clothing brands. Often, the brand name will be prominently displayed on the garments themselves, making the wearer a walking advertisement for the product and a testament to its popularity.

The appeal to the desire for love is also very powerful in the political sphere, where it is closely related to the bandwagon technique. A campaign may project the impression that a candidate's popularity will transfer to all those who join his or her bandwagon.

In the 2004 Democratic primary, John Kerry started out with the support of only about 9% of Democrats. After his surprise victory in the Iowa caucus, however, he polled at around 50%. Kerry's popularity increased even further, going up to about 68% of Democrats, after his subsequent victory in the New Hampshire primary. Surveys show that name recognition went up very little—indicating that people changed their minds largely because of the results of early primaries.

Many activist groups have also harnessed the desire for popularity in order to help promote their causes. Environmental groups, animal rights groups, social movements, and others have successfully transformed their causes into trendy social phenomena. For example, over the last decade, environmental groups have made a strong and intentional push to make conspicuous consumption unpopular. Their propaganda efforts have emphasized recycling and vegetarianism, and the conservation of water, electricity, and fossil fuels. These behaviors, identified as "green," carry a certain social cachet.

A recycling campaign features two young, attractive environmentalists walking through a forest of smiling trees, with the caption: "Love Nature, and Nature will love you back."

People want to feel that they are loved on an individual level, and propaganda can make use of that desire. For example, political propaganda in totalitarian governments often fosters a familial relationship between citizens and the state. By assuming a parental attitude, a government may gain the kind of trust and loyalty usually reserved for family members.

Use of the word "comrade," in the former Soviet Union made each citizen feel like part of an alliance of friends, fighting for a better world.

Propagandists exploit the desire for love to promote everything from cologne to communism. These messages are most harmful, however, when the sender of the message wants not only a few dollars of market share, but also power—when the action you are being encouraged to perform is not merely buying Brand X instead of Brand Y, but making a life-changing, possibly life-threatening decision. In such cases, it is best to let reason hold sway over desire.

THE FEAR OF REJECTION

Desire works by pulling us toward something, often encouraging us to disengage our rational minds and become overwhelmed with feelings. Fear also disengages the rational mind, but it does so by arousing a sense of panic. The desire for popularity makes us embrace a product or idea to gain acceptance, while a fear of rejection may cause us to clutch at it, for fear of being ostracized.

While not everyone cares about being in the in-group, no one wants to be totally left out. Marketers know this fact and play on this fear when attempting to sell their products. Advertisements for diets, make-up, cosmetic surgery, clothing, and exercise programs often try to promote feelings of anxiety and a negative self-image. Then, once they have convinced people that they are at risk of being rejected, these propagandists offer a simple solution in the form of a product.

The 1923 ad campaign for a popular mouthwash relied on the tag line, "always a bridesmaid, never a bride," implying that the reason some women were not married was bad breath, which the product claimed to fix.

Similarly, political propaganda often encourages a fear of being rejected or left behind. A campaign may put forth a progressive, energetic image and suggest that, should you fail to jump on board right away, you may find yourself embarrassingly out of step with the rest of society. As you can tell, preying on the fear of rejection often involves the use of the false-dilemma technique: you're either with us or against us, and to be against us is to be alone.

Propagandists often create a sense of superiority and exclusivity based on a certain behavior, belief, or status. Once members of a group have been encouraged to feel superior to the rest of the world, they can be controlled by the threat of becoming outcasts. As long as group membership is built on following the right rules, buying the right product, or supporting the right leaders, group membership can be rescinded and members can be controlled by fear.

Just as the exploitation of a person's desire to be loved and popular is related to the bandwagon technique, the exploitation of the fear of rejection is related to name-calling. When you are rejected, excluded, excommunicated, shunned, or condemned, you become the outsider, the "other."

The desire for love and the fear of rejection are powerful motivators in an increasingly impersonal world.

CHAPTER 14: THE DESIRE FOR PROSPERITY AND THE FEAR OF POWERLESSNESS

Almost as strong as the desire for love is the drive to acquire material possessions and power. From a longing to control vast numbers of people to the enjoyment of knowing a waiter will tend to your every request, most people are enticed by the idea of a secure and privileged lifestyle. Likewise, of course, we are easily motivated by the fear of losing our wealth, our privilege, or our safety. In this chapter, we'll discuss the different ways in which propagandists can use these related desires and fears to control our thoughts and actions.

THE DESIRE FOR PROSPERITY

Perhaps the most reasonable desire for power is the longing to control one's own life. The fast pace of the modern world often leaves people feeling completely out of control, and anything that offers to help them manage their lives is appealing.

An ad campaign depicts a man whose life is transformed by the purchase of a particular brand of deodorant. Once weak and indecisive, he is now able to make decisions with confidence and strength.

As unrealistic as such claims may seem, propaganda often exploits the desire for prosperity by claiming that a prescribed action, product, or service will give you a taste of power or a better life.

A series of credit card advertisements portrays a card owner exercising power over valets, waiters, caddies, airline attendants, and others in the service industry simply by wielding this particular card.

In politics, this desire is often exploited to promote a particular candidate. For instance, in 1928, Herbert Hoover convinced people to vote for him by promising prosperity in the form of "a chicken in every pot and a car in every garage." Similarly, propaganda can be used to make people believe that a particular candidate will empower them. Jesse Jackson's speech at the 1988 Democratic National Convention is a prime example of this kind of message:

> *"When we form a great quilt of unity and common ground, we'll have the power to bring about health care and housing and jobs and education and hope to our Nation. We, the people, can win!"*

Often, appeals to the desire for strength and control are particularly effective when aimed at groups that have been oppressed in one way or another. The famous, "Rosie the Riveter," for instance, called American women to join the work force with the emboldening message, "We can do it!" This propaganda poster, promising power and influence to American women, was so popular that it resurfaced as a rallying call for the feminist movement of the 1960s and 1970s.

The familiar WWII figure of "Rosie the Riveter" has been used as an icon of American strength and determination, and as a symbol of feminism.

When the promise of wealth, security, or power has little or nothing to do with the proposed action, you're probably looking at propaganda. In the example that follows, the propagandist claims that nuclear war will lead to prosperity. This is an excellent example of an attempt to bypass logic by appealing to desire.

This poster promotes "total war," or nuclear holocaust, by depicting the aftermath as a clean, peaceful, and prosperous world.

THE FEAR OF POWERLESSNESS

As strong as the desire for prosperity can be, there are times when the appeal to fear is a more effective tool. The fear of losing power, resources, and security is a factor in many propaganda campaigns that rely more on feelings than on logic. Often, this style of propaganda appeals to the fear of losing one's material wealth and possessions.

Sometimes, this type of propaganda can appeal to outright selfishness. In the following example, the Nazi government advocates the elimination of the disabled by appealing to the fear of financial loss.

*This poster, supporting Nazi eugenics studies, preys on the fear of having one's
resources wasted. It reads: "This person, suffering from hereditary defects,
will cost society 60,000 German marks over his lifetime. People, that is your
money! Read New People, the journal of the Office of Racial Politics of the
Nazi Party."*

However, in some cases, propagandists appeal to less materialistic fears. The
fear of losing the power to protect one's family is a powerful motivator, often used in
times of war.

The poster above exploits the fear of letting one's family come to harm. This particular fear was exploited very well during WWII, and much of the propaganda from this time depicts frightened, helpless children.

As we've seen in this chapter, propaganda often uses promises and threats to prompt people to action. Often, however, the actions prescribed are only loosely related to the benefit or danger the propagandist describes. An individual's decision to buy war bonds will not directly protect children from harm, just as supporting "total war" has no clear connection to future prosperity. These arguments appeal to human emotions, but they do not stand up to the test of logic.

> The desire for power and prosperity and the fear of
> loss are two of the sentiments propagandists exploit to
> bypass rational thought.

CHAPTER 15: THE DESIRE FOR IMMORTALITY AND THE FEAR OF DEATH

The fear of death and the desire for immortality are very closely related. In both cases, continued life is the desired outcome, and death is to be avoided. Depending on the circumstances, however, one way of stating the issue may be considerably more powerful than the other.

In the case of an anti-smoking campaign, for instance, preying on the fear of death is far more appropriate than promising health and longevity. After all, a person who doesn't smoke will not necessarily live to an old age, so the advertiser cannot promise a long life to those who don't smoke. In an ad for a "healthy" breakfast cereal, on the other hand, it would make more sense to appeal to the audience's desire for a long life. In any case, a company cannot claim that failing to eat its cereal causes death.

DESIRE FOR LONGEVITY

Advertising that plays up to the desire for longevity can be found everywhere. Many advertisers depict only the fittest, healthiest-looking people using their products. An athletic shoe, worn by a slim, energetic jogger, may be marketed as the key to fitness. A granola bar may be advertised as the snack choice of an active young couple on a camping trip. Through ads like these, we are encouraged to believe that if we use these products, we, too, will always be fit and healthy. Using the transfer technique, these ads associate the health and vitality of these individuals with the products they are advertising.

There is an emphasis on youth in many such advertisements, and audiences are encouraged to believe that perpetual youth is an achievable goal, with the right product or service. This technique is especially common in the advertisement of beauty products.

You'll look and feel ten years younger.

However, even a travel agency may appeal to the desire for longevity, claiming that a Caribbean cruise will, "wash away the years," and "make you young again."

The desire for immortality is an effective tool for advertisers, but it can also be useful for activists and politicians who want to promote public involvement in a movement or cause. Ideals, nations, and political systems outlive individual human beings. Hence, people can be lead to believe that they are gaining some form of immortality by supporting a cause that will outlive them and improve the lives of future generations.

Help preserve the wetlands—for a greener tomorrow.

FEAR OF DEATH

There is no stronger motivator than the fear of death, so it is no surprise that propaganda frequently targets this fear. While you might expect so intense a threat to be used only in drastic propaganda campaigns, it is actually used for a variety of purposes. In advertising, this fear is most often used to promote products or services that can reduce the risk of death.

Our luxury sedan now comes with side and rear airbags. It has been tested in more than a thousand crashes to make sure that you and your loved ones are safe, no matter what.

In times of war, the fear of death is used widely in government propaganda. Particularly when the danger seems remote, bringing the fear of death home to the citizens is important in garnering support for the war effort. During the Cold War, for example, it was important that Americans be reminded regularly that the Soviet Union could, at any moment, attack the United States and kill millions. Regular school drills prepared students for a nuclear attack, citizens were instructed on the proper disposal of radioactive fallout, and shelters were erected to make the public aware of the dire threat posed by the Soviet Union.

In a series of survival pamphlets put out by the Civil Defense Office, the US government played upon citizens' fears, even while spreading potentially helpful information. Such an "information campaign" might have been genuinely helpful in preparing citizens to face potential dangers, but it also served the secondary function of gaining support for the Cold War initiatives of the United States.

TEMPORARY BASEMENT FALLOUT SHELTER

There is no escaping the fact that nuclear conflict would leave a tragic world ... The experience would be terrible beyond imagination and description ... There are no total answers, no easy answers, no cheap answers to the question of protection from nuclear attack. But there are answers. Some of them are in this booklet. —Fallout Protection, 1961

With their fears aroused, people are much more supportive of whatever action is deemed necessary to protect their lives—including military spending, secret government programs, and hard-line diplomatic tactics. This tactic was used during the Vietnam War in the form of "The Domino Theory." According to this premise, used to justify US involvement in the war, if the US allowed the Communists to conquer Vietnam, the rest of Southeast Asia would soon fall to them, and, eventually, the United States would have to fight Communists on American soil.

The fear of death can also be used outside of wartime propaganda. By encouraging a fear of terrorist attacks on airlines, for example, officials are better able to justify heightened security precautions. Although people might naturally be reluctant to accept inconveniences, once sufficiently frightened by the threat of death, citizens become more accommodating.

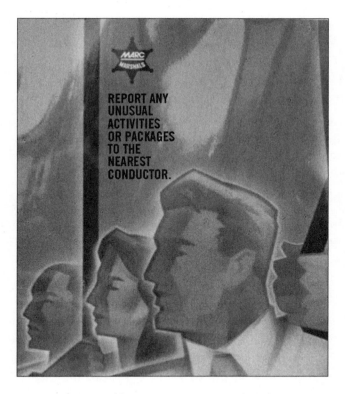

This poster suggests to public transit passengers that danger is imminent. From here, it will be easier to convince passengers to put up with increased security precautions and modify other behaviors, if necessary.

The underlying message in propaganda that exploits the fear of death is often simply, "support us, or you will probably die." When faced with the prospect of death, people are less inclined toward rational thought. All other concerns, including a thorough, rational investigation of the propagandist's claims, are secondary to survival.

A campaign showing the potentially deadly effects of E. coli contamination leaves people wondering if this deadly bacterium is lurking in their fresh spinach or lettuce. Symptoms are listed. Death from E. coli infections is described. Millions of people stop eating foods that could be contaminated, and restaurants and grocery stores stop selling them. Nevertheless, the chances of dying of E. coli poisoning from fresh vegetables are actually infinitesimally small.

At the same time, the American Heart Association continues an ongoing campaign to educate people about heart health, recommending an exercise regimen and diet modifications. But, while heart disease is a leading cause of death in the US, it takes a long time to kill people. Relatively simple actions suggested by the AHA are ignored. The same high-cholesterol diets and inactive lifestyles are followed. Millions of people continue to die each year of heart disease.

Both of these health-related campaigns make use of the fear of death, but one makes the threat seem more frightening, more of a hidden killer lurking in the shadows. As a result, people are far more worried about E. coli than heart disease—even though, statistically, heart disease poses a far greater threat.

Separating the emotional hype from the facts helps you to make rational decisions about how you want to act. Putting the fear of death aside and addressing each concern in a calm, logical manner helps to ensure that you make the best decisions.

> **One of the most powerful motivators is the fear of death. Hence, it stands to reason that among the most universal longings is the desire for a long life, or even immortality. Propagandists frequently appeal to both of these related feelings.**

CHAPTER 16:
POSITIVE USES OF PROPAGANDA

The word *propaganda* has strong negative connotations in the modern world. Even in this book, we've focused primarily on its destructive uses because it's important to be on guard against the dangers propaganda poses. However, that doesn't mean that propaganda cannot be used for good. Like most tools, propaganda is not necessarily evil, in and of itself. It is true that manipulative advertisers and unscrupulous politicians can use propaganda to suit their own ends. But propaganda can also help to end slavery, promote peace, or encourage people to improve their world.

In the following chapters, we'll look at some examples of how propaganda can be used to inspire constructive and positive actions. In addition to promoting strife and conflict, propaganda can also be used to encourage and inspire.

Determining whether intentional manipulation through propaganda is ever justified is a complicated matter. Some do not approve of its use in any situation, while others maintain that the ends can sometimes justify the means. Ultimately, however, the decision is yours to make.

Propaganda is not always used for destructive purposes; some would even say that propaganda is often beneficial.

CHAPTER 17: EVOKING SYMPATHY AND INSPIRING GENEROSITY

One of the most positive ways propaganda can be used is inspiring sympathy: encouraging people to share in someone else's suffering. Sympathy is a very useful tool for the propagandist and for people in general. Understanding what others are feeling helps us relate to others and allows us to function in a community. A propagandist knows just how to trigger these compassionate feelings and use them to gain an advantage.

Many factors can help activate feelings of sympathy and empathy. For example, we tend to feel more sympathy for close relatives. This may have to do, in part, with an instinct to help preserve our genes. It may be connected to the amount of time we spend with family. Or, it may simply be part of an individual's personality. We also tend to feel more sympathy for people who remind us of ourselves. When people are like us, it is easier to put ourselves in their position and empathize with them. People who are perceived as underdogs also tend to inspire sympathy, while the powerful—especially if they seem smug in that power—are much more difficult to pity.

These three factors that increase sympathy—relation, similarity, and status—serve as starting points for the propagandist. He or she may try to highlight any or all of these factors to increase audience sympathy.

This photograph was part of a 1935 project commissioned by the Farm Security Administration. In an effort to prove the necessity of Roosevelt's "New Deal," photographers documented the living conditions of impoverished rural America during the Great Depression. This image appeals to an audience's sympathy by portraying an average American family in distress.

It is often difficult to sympathize with people who are perceived as outsiders. We may find it hard to muster enthusiasm about helping people who seem "different" from us in terms of ethnicity, religion, economic status, physical appearance, etc. For most of us, there are simply too many people in the world to be highly sympathetic to all of them.

Imagine how you would feel if a loved one were in pain— perhaps sick with cancer. Your sympathy would have no bounds. Now, imagine having the same emotional response for every person in the world who suffers from cancer. This kind of sympathy would make life unlivable. By necessity, we separate ourselves from people we do not know directly. Envision concentric circles radiating out from you, with your sympathetic response becoming less intense with each circle. Of course, that isn't to say that you do not feel sympathy for people far removed from you; your response to their troubles may simply be less intense than what you feel for a relative, possibly because there is nothing you could do to help.

A propagandist who wants to arouse sympathy for a person or group that seems distant must find a way to make you think of that person as inhabiting a closer circle. The easiest way to do this is to highlight commonalities. Finding similarities with other people encourages us to be more sympathetic. Fellow fans of a sports team, members of our religion or political party, schoolmates, players of the same online game—these are all people we can relate to. When we find out that a person belongs to our group, our sympathies are affected.

We might hear about a person who was in a fatal car accident and shrug it off as one of many horrible things that happen every day. But, when we find out that he or she went to our school, there is a much stronger emotional impact. Likewise, we might receive a flyer soliciting donations for a family whose home was devastated by a hurricane and throw the paper away. We might justify such inaction by reasoning that we cannot possibly help everyone. However, if we should learn that this family once lived in our hometown, we may find it in our hearts to donate to their cause. From an objective standpoint, nothing about the situation has changed; nevertheless, our reaction has changed, dramatically.

Every shared characteristic makes it that much easier to relate to a person or group, and every difference makes relating that much more difficult. Hence, propagandists emphasize similarities. One of the simplest ways a propagandist can show similarity is by highlighting our shared humanity.

For example, a propagandist may say, "Throughout Africa, millions of people are starving. Your donation will help feed Africa." However, it is difficult to relate to nameless, faceless people half a world away; their anonymity makes them easy to ignore. A good propaganda campaign will, instead, focus on the humanity of one or a handful of people, pointing to our shared traits to help us associate ourselves more closely with those in need. Notice the difference in the two images that follow. Which one arouses more sympathy?

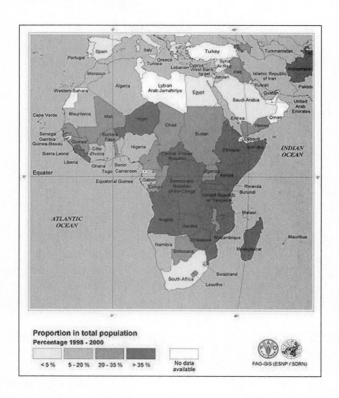

"Little Eric is ten years old. Every morning he wakes up, unsure if he will be eating that day. Every night he goes to bed praying that the next day might bring relief to his hunger. Give today and help feed Eric and the millions like him throughout Africa."

Some propaganda campaigns get even more specific about shared traits. A campaign designed to raise awareness about injured veterans from a country's most recent war, for example, will probably be most effective when targeting older veterans. The shared experience of fighting a war helps encourage a greater level of sympathy.

Equally effective in promoting sympathy is the appeal of the underdog. People are most likely to feel sympathy for someone who appears to be in trouble. There are numerous situations in which "playing the underdog" would be inappropriate; a struggling investment company, for instance, is not an attractive prospect. In the right situations, however, promoting this type of image is a powerful way to evoke sympathy.

Establishing underdog status is often simply a matter of properly handling one's image. Although it might be hard to think of a millionaire as an underdog, many political campaigns have accomplished just such an image for their wealthy, privileged candidates, through skillful propaganda. Presenting the person as fighting against great odds, battling a monolithic foe, or consistently triumphing when least expected all help to establish underdog status. However, finding the fine line between being an object of sympathy and an object of pity can be a tricky task for the propagandist. People are sometimes repulsed by people they pity, which can undermine a propagandist's aims. If used correctly, however, the underdog method can be enormously successful, giving the public an impetus for action.

INSPIRING GENEROSITY

Much of the benevolent propaganda in the modern world is aimed at encouraging generosity. To this end, propagandists often attempt to make people aware of their own wealth. If people think of themselves as poor, without much to spare, it is much more difficult to convince them to be generous. If, on the other hand, they are encouraged to see themselves as having privileges beyond most people, generosity can be inspired more easily.

For the price of a new CD, you can ensure that Eric's family has clean drinking water for the year.

Convincing people of their privileged status can take two distinct forms. The gentler form is to simply show people how lucky they are to have as much as they do and to show them that others in the world are not so blessed. This is best achieved through a nonconfrontational approach aimed at inducing sympathy and magnanimity. The less gentle form is to show people their own affluence in a way that inspires guilt. This technique is widely seen in propaganda campaigns targeting prosperous Westerners. Many in the West are predisposed to feel guilty about their relative wealth, and, by targeting those pre-existing feelings, propagandists make a strong case for charitable giving.

Once these feelings have been aroused, it's important to convince the individual that his or her individual contribution is vital. Although we may feel a desire to give, it is easy to justify not giving by telling ourselves that there are millions of people already contributing to the cause in question. If we do not feel that our assistance is needed, we probably won't take action. Propagandists address this problem by speaking directly to their audience members and letting them know how much they are needed. Often, they create the impression that without *your* support, the entire endeavor will fail. Although this is very rarely true in a literal sense, being singled out makes people more willing to give.

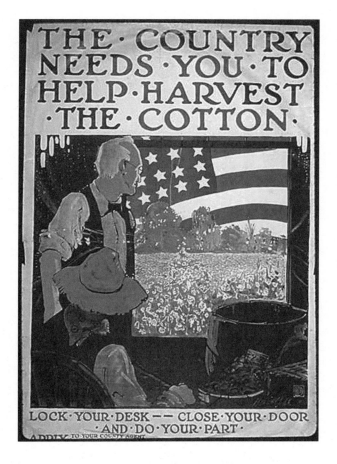

Propagandists know that people like to feel that they are at the center of the universe, and they exploit this tendency toward egocentrism. For this reason, both political and marketing campaigns often use this tactic to great effect, addressing the recipient by name and using phrases such as:

"You can make a difference."

and

"We need your help now."

There is a sense of urgency in these phrases, and they convey the feeling that the propagandist is speaking directly to you—as if you are the only one in the world who can make a difference.

A third technique used to inspire generosity is to emphasize the virtue of charity. This technique capitalizes on the fact that most people are taught that it is commendable, or even a moral imperative, to care for those in need. Good propaganda reinforces this idea, and promises its audience the feeling of generosity and virtue.

People who subscribe to a religious belief system may be reminded of the hypocrisy of supporting charity through words, but not through deeds.

Charitable propaganda also makes extensive use of simple assertions, flooding the public with various messages through direct mailing campaigns, billboards, and commercials. Because marketers do not expect to have your attention for very long, the assertions are often short and direct, with no explanations or justifications.

Since you started reading this, 300 children have died of starvation. Without your immediate help, thousands more will die. Call now.

The testimonial technique is also frequently used in campaigns for charitable giving. High-profile celebrities are brought on board to lend their faces and voices to a cause. The propagandists subtly suggest that you can be more like these rich, famous, and beautiful people if you give to the cause at hand, encouraging you to jump on the bandwagon of sympathy and generosity.

While many people are unhappy when they discover they've been manipulated by a mainstream advertising campaign, they may not mind being subjected to the same techniques for a cause they support. One might say they have been tricked into doing something good. However, even nonprofit organizations can misappropriate donations. Some leading nonprofit executives earn rather lucrative salaries. Moreover, in some cases, the funds they raise may go into a general pool where they can be used by affiliated organizations—even those that donators may not support.

There are certainly ways of kindling generosity in people through rational discourse, without resorting to propagandistic techniques, but the propagandist asks you to follow your emotions. While this may prove a more effective form of persuasion, some consider it unethical. Each of the approaches discussed in this chapter can be viewed as manipulative, and whether it is appropriate to use such tools to encourage even a benevolent end is a question well worth considering.

Despite its negative reputation, propaganda has often been used to inspire selfless acts of compassion and charity.

CHAPTER 18:
PROMOTING CIVIC RESPONSIBILITY

Like the appeals to sympathy and generosity, the appeal to civic-mindedness attempts to capitalize on benevolent feelings. In this case, the benevolent feelings are zeroed in on a community, be it a neighborhood, a state, or even a planet.

To be *civic-minded* is to be concerned for the welfare of the community. It is what often keeps us from throwing garbage on the ground and what leads us to volunteer to help organize a parade for our local youth. Like sympathy and generosity, civic-mindedness can be encouraged through propaganda. Most communities, whether large or small, spend at least some time and money on fostering a sense of community and making citizens aware of community issues.

Because Western societies tend to be quite individualistic, it is easy for us to neglect civic responsibilities that, in other cultures, would be impossible to ignore. Reaffirming our part in the larger social scheme, therefore, plays an important role in building a campaign of civic-mindedness. On the local level, building this sort of understanding usually involves direct appeals from leaders in the community. Politicians, church leaders, and the heads of philanthropic organizations are all solicited for testimonials aimed at building a sense of community responsibility.

On the state and national level, fostering a sense of community can be more difficult. It is hard to feel like an important part of a nation, for example, when you are only one among millions. Again, finding high-profile personalities to endorse civic responsibility is one of the most effective techniques. At this level, such endorsements usually come from well-known politicians or celebrities. Citizens are given a model to emulate—a hero to associate with the cause at hand. In some cases, they may even begin to feel that they are accountable to that familiar figure. At both the local and national levels, the underlying message remains the same: you are a small, but vital, part of the organization.

Another way of encouraging citizens to uphold their duties is by appealing to individual selfishness. For instance, consider a common argument used to encourage children not to pick up shells from a beach: if everyone took one shell, there would be none left on the beach. Such arguments, however compelling, are based on flawed logic. In reality, if one person fails to take shells, that doesn't necessarily mean that no one else will take shells—and, conversely, if one person does take shells, that doesn't mean that everyone else will. In truth, there is no causal relationship between the two. Likewise, in the community at large, scores of people who do not fulfill their civic duties continually reap the benefits of other people's hard work.

But the fact that this argument is based on a logical fallacy doesn't mean that it isn't effective—it simply means that it's propaganda. It is, in fact, a very effective way to make people undertake unpleasant civic duties. Many people attend jury duty, for example, because they want their peers to do likewise. Paying taxes, helping at a child's school, volunteering for projects at work—this same mentality plays a role in each of these actions.

Engaging in behaviors that help the community can be a very gratifying personal experience. The propagandist can play up this sense of fulfillment to encourage people to engage in their communities. Even before people act, the mere feeling of belonging tends to make them feel good about themselves. The feeling of caring for and belonging to one's community is immensely satisfying to many people.

学习潘冬子 做党的好孩子

The above image, from the Chinese revolutionary period, portrays people who do their part for the Communist party as happy and fulfilled.

Many propaganda campaigns that are meant to encourage civic-mindedness include a bandwagon appeal. Posters looking for people to help with any sort of community service, for example, will often depict groups of friendly, happy looking individuals. Big smiles, an obvious sense of teamwork, and overall satisfaction permeate the images of civic propaganda. This can be seen most dramatically in the large-scale civic propaganda campaigns of Communist China and Russia, in which the people assisting the community all look incredibly happy. When targeting groups that are suffering and unhappy, the images of fulfillment and friendship can be particularly compelling.

One specific kind of civic responsibility often encouraged through propaganda is voting. Most political campaigns are meant to attract voters to a particular candidate, but there is also propaganda that promotes voting for anyone at all. Most nations that consider themselves democratic allow their citizens to choose whether they want to take part in elections, and not everyone will choose to participate—in the United States, only about 50% of the population votes, on average.

This advertisement encourages people to vote without endorsing a particular candidate or party.

Fear and guilt are two emotions that can be used effectively in motivating people to vote. Fear is a strong motivator in general, and when something as important as the leadership of one's country is in question, it can be particularly powerful. Perhaps one of the most effective uses of fear is to make members of one group feel that, if they do not turn out to vote, a rival group will take over the country. Imagine an election in which one ethnic group is threatened with the suggestion that another ethnic group will turn out in large numbers that year, or older voters threatened with the number of young voters slated to participate in the election.

In a similar approach, guilt can also be used as a strong motivator. Showing people the negative consequences of failing to vote is one way to combine fear and guilt. People who dislike their city council member, for example, might be told that if they had voted in the previous election, she wouldn't have been elected. The burden of that council member's negative policies is placed on the citizens' shoulders. At the next election, this guilt is used to ensure that they show up—for fear that they will be held responsible for the election of another politician they dislike.

In the last six years, our city streets have fallen into disrepair. Crime has risen by 6%. Unemployment has continued to grow. In the last election, your voice was not heard, and, for many, your silence has led to despair. Make sure you are heard. Make the next six years count.

Of course, not all voting-related propaganda uses fear and guilt to motivate people. Whatever your political affiliation, this propaganda tells us, on election day, we are all united, fulfilling our civic duty and upholding democracy. A propagandist can appeal to this sense of pride by bringing up a nation's history and legacy, by reminding us of the ideals people fought and died for, and by comparing our government with oppressive systems throughout the world.

Voters are given stickers that proclaim, "I Voted!" The unspoken question is, "Why haven't you?"

This sense of duty and pride is particularly effective against those who feel that they have a vested interest in the democratic system. When propaganda campaigns target war veterans, for example, they rely heavily on this sentiment to get voters to the polls. Since these men and women fought and may have sacrificed a great deal to defend the ideal of democracy, they are receptive to the suggestion that voting is a way of upholding that ideal.

Another category of action that is often promoted as a civic duty is supporting a nation's war efforts. Some of the most memorable propaganda campaigns in United States history, launched during World War I and World War II, were designed for just that purpose. There were three major fronts to these campaigns: the selling of war bonds, the rationing of resources, and the recruitment of service men and women.

The campaign to sell war bonds was incredibly pervasive during World War I and World War II. Both wars were extraordinarily expensive for the United States, and the military budget was not nearly so large as it is today. The only way the wars could be waged successfully was with direct financial support from the American people.

During both World Wars, propagandists presented buying war bonds as a duty, not merely as a good deed.

To put the need into perspective, consider the fact that in 1913, the United States spent less than $1 billion on all of its expenses combined. By comparison, in 1917 and 1918, the war effort alone cost more than $30 billion. It is no surprise, then, that a massive propaganda campaign would be focused on the sale of war bonds through a combination of appeals to patriotism, fear, obligation, and the bandwagon phenomenon. During WWII, celebrity testimonials were also used quite successfully to get people to support the war effort. Famous people, from President Roosevelt to Rita Hayworth, made their personal contributions public to encourage Americans to support the war effort.

Movie star Rita Hayworth encourages Americans to contribute scrap metal for World War II by posing with a car whose bumper has been donated.

One important step the wartime propagandists took during World Wars I and II was changing the way people thought about buying bonds. Rather than portraying it as an option one could choose to take, propagandists described buying bonds as a responsibility of every American.

In fact, this message was so effective that groups that opposed the wars—most notably the National Service Board for Religious Objectors—still took part in the bond-selling effort. Various pacifist churches offered "civilian bonds," as an alternative for people who felt the need to support their country, while protesting the war itself.

Beyond merely buying war bonds, people were also asked to ration various materials that the war effort required.

Since there was a limited supply of food, gasoline, and certain metals, it was important that consumer demand stay low, so that the government could acquire all it needed to keep the war machine running smoothly. People from all walks of life were asked to make daily sacrifices to ensure that there were enough resources for the troops abroad.

In addition to financial support and rationing, the war efforts of World War I and World War II also required the enlistment of military personnel. US armed forces were made up entirely of volunteers at that time, and many troops were needed. Propaganda played an important role in recruiting the necessary number of troops. Meanwhile, at home, industrial manufacturing had increased immensely, to produce battleships, guns, tanks, bombs, and other supplies. Since the majority of workers had been shipped overseas to fight in the war, there weren't nearly enough men to operate the factories. Hence, propaganda was also used to convince women to take factory jobs that had been exclusively held by men before the war.

This propaganda poster encourages American women to view factory work as a suitable occupation for a woman, while promoting the sale of bonds.

During World War I, much of the enlistment propaganda focused on downplaying the dangers of battle, while at the same time romanticizing the war. World War I was incredibly bloody, and a soldier's chance of death or severe injury was quite high. Nevertheless, most of the propaganda of the era depicted fighting the war as an ordinary, everyday job. By focusing on the more positive aspects of war, the messages ensured that people wouldn't think about the possibility of death or mutilation. Instead, they were free to focus on helping their country and being thought of as heroes.

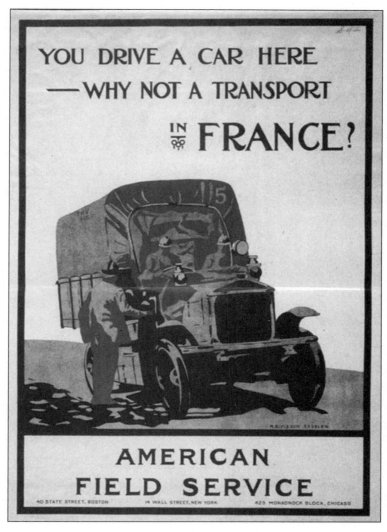

This poster equates field service with an ordinary day's work.

Evocative images were used in the propaganda of both wars. The deaths of American troops were used as a way to incite people to take action.

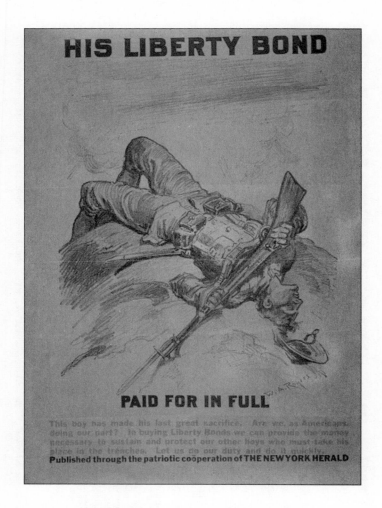

*Images of fallen soldiers elicit sadness, anger, frustration, and guilt—
emotions meant to inspire people to take action.*

This was particularly true of World War II propaganda, in which references to
Pearl Harbor were frequently used to inspire Americans with a sense of duty and a
desire for vengeance.

During World War II, images of troops in battle, airplanes dropping bombs on Germany, and German and American troops clashing encouraged Americans to view combat in a romantic light. In these situations, propaganda inspired people to make sacrifices for the good of the nation.

When used skillfully and responsibly, propaganda can encourage a variety of altruistic actions that can improve our communities and our world. However, when used irresponsibly, propaganda can inspire some of the greatest atrocities imaginable. Now that we have discussed some of propaganda's more positive uses, we will go on to discuss just how dangerous propaganda can be, at its worst.

It is always a wise idea to examine what you're being asked to do in the name of civic responsibility; think critically about the motives and the logic behind the messages you see and hear.

CHAPTER 19:
NEGATIVE USES OF PROPAGANDA

Not all propaganda can be qualified as simply "good" or "bad." To categorize it as such would be an oversimplification. Individuals have diverse opinions on the subject of what, if anything, constitutes "good" propaganda, and what, if anything, can be called strictly "bad." For instance, is it wrong for an advertiser to try to make people want to take a vacation? What about making them want to spend their vacation gambling? How about if you try to get them to spend every penny they own at your casino? At what point does propaganda cross the line, going from benign to harmful?

Most of the propaganda you encounter in ordinary circumstances is not overtly destructive. However, in some instances, propaganda has caused pain, suffering, and death for countless people. These are the kinds of campaigns that most would consider harmful and inhumane. You may find many of them disturbing. However, by learning about mistakes people have made in the past, we can be better equipped to make decisions in the present.

We'll begin by talking about the specific emotions propagandists often use in bringing about turmoil and strife. Fear, anger, hatred—all of these feelings are widely used by propagandists for their individual purposes. After all, when we have lost ourselves in such emotions, we are more inclined to accept the simplest answer, the most convenient cure, or the most impressive hero that comes along.

Propaganda that has destructive intentions often begins by inspiring negative emotions.

CHAPTER 20:
PROVOKING FEAR AND HOSTILITY

As previously discussed, fear is one of the most powerful motivators—and for good reason. When we are afraid, we often respond with a fight-or-flight reaction that allows us to make split-second, life-saving decisions. The fear reaction allows us to dodge speeding cars and defend ourselves from animal attacks. However, in a panicked state of mind, we often lose much of our capacity for rational thought. While fear may be helpful in situations of physical danger, it is not the ideal state of mind for making complex decisions.

The things people are most afraid of—disease, crime, economic collapse, and other calamities—are usually complicated issues, with complex causes and solutions. Our rational minds should be operating at maximum capacity when dealing with such issues, not shutting down to let our emotions take over. But, it is easy to be overwhelmed with feelings, and propagandists depend on this emotional response when they try to evoke fear in people they want to manipulate.

Different cultures and different eras have been dominated by different fears. In twenty-first century America, for example, concerns about security are a powerful motivator. Think of all the ways in which propaganda in the modern age tells you that your security is tenuous and attack is imminent from all directions. Terrorists may be planning their next attack on innocent civilians. Someone may be stealing your identity and ruining your credit. The world's supply of oil is running out, so you may not be able to drive in the near future. The world is heating up, and the ice caps are melting, so your house may soon be under water. Your children may be abducted and murdered. Your house may be destroyed in a horrible fire, earthquake, or flood, and you may wind up homeless.

Today, all a thief needs is your name and address to take your most precious possession… your identity.

We are bombarded by almost constant threats. The phrase "culture of fear" has been used to describe this atmosphere of unease and distrust, in which the everyday vagaries of the world seem to threaten our very lives.

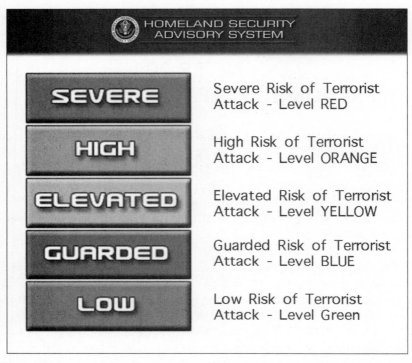

A system such as the US Threat Level Advisory System, put in effect after the terrorist attacks of September 11th, may help reduce the danger of terrorist attacks, but critics have accused it of contributing to the "culture of fear." They argue that people are kept in a constant state of anxiety by such vague warnings of danger.

Creating a general climate of fear can prepare the public to accept further propaganda. Always worried about our safety, we are ready to believe the worst about anything. In this environment, it doesn't take much work to make something harmless suddenly seem terrifying. Even common household items and foods, from lead-painted toys to contaminated beef, can suddenly become life-threatening menaces. There is a constant sense of apprehension, and it seems that threats to our safety are lurking in our midst at all times.

The propaganda that contributes to this constant anxiety makes additional propaganda even more effective. Rather than growing skeptical about such threats, most people become more susceptible to further fear-inspiring messages.

The fear aroused by propaganda is often disproportionate to the actual danger. Nevertheless, people will often accept horrible conditions when presented with the lesser-of-two-evils technique.

"The streets of our country are in turmoil. The universities are filled with students rebelling and rioting. Communists are seeking to destroy our country. Russia is threatening us with her might, and the Republic is in danger. Yes—danger from within and without. We need law and order! Without it, our nation cannot survive." —Adolf Hitler, in support of his fascist regime

The next time you're exposed to a message that arouses fear, be sure to look at it critically. Dig beneath the surface and evaluate how accurate the message is. Is the threat being exaggerated? Ask yourself how much of your fear comes from the actual danger, and how much is based on the presentation. If you're being asked to take an action, is there any reason to believe that taking that action will reduce the danger? Planes seem much more terrifying to us than cars, even though we may know that cars are, statistically, much more likely to cause death. The most important step in overcoming this type of propaganda is to understand how it works and to reengage your rational mind. Once our fears are subdued and logic is reintroduced, we can see the situation for what it really is.

ANGER

Anger is closely related to fear and can be used to much the same effect. In fact, anger often grows from feelings of fear or uncertainty. Anger is also a very common reaction to injustice, humiliation, or betrayal. Like most negative emotions, the main utility of anger for a propagandist is its capacity to shut down all rational thought. People often speak of 'seeing red' when angry and losing the ability to control their actions.

When faced with a message that inspires anger, it is best to evaluate the logic behind it and look for evidence of ulterior motives. Often, simply taking the time to assess a message from a rational viewpoint is enough to make anger subside. With emotions in check, we are free to look at the situation in a rational light and determine the most appropriate reaction.

As with positive propaganda, there are times when negative propaganda is used to evoke emotions only; at other times, however, negative emotions are used as a first step toward inciting a specific, hostile action.

HATRED AND DISTRUST

Hatred, like fear, is a powerful motivator of human actions. Where hate exists, the road to violence, theft, or nearly any atrocity is well paved. Hatred allows us to dehumanize another person or group and can serve as justification for any action we might want to take. Once a propagandist has established hate within the target audience, he or she can steer people quite easily in the desired direction. While hatred is an extreme feeling of enmity, distrust is a wary, uncertain feeling. When people distrust another person or group, they are constantly looking for faults or missteps.

The greatness of every mighty organization embodying an idea in this world lies in the religious fanaticism and intolerance with which, fanatically convinced of its own right, it intolerantly imposes its will against all others." —This quote from Adolf Hitler's *Mein Kampf* celebrates intolerance as a virtue.

Usually developing from emotions like fear and anger, hate and distrust reduce a person's ability to reason. Once these feelings have been aroused, a propagandist need only present us with a target for our negative emotions—an object for our hatred. A propaganda campaign might take something we feel is necessary to our survival and portray a particular group or individual as threatening that necessity. Thus, the audience fixes its fear and anger on a single, hated object.

For example, most Americans consider choosing one's job to be an indispensable freedom. So, during the 1950s, Communists were portrayed as wanting to take that right away from Americans, by having jobs assigned by the state. Regardless of whether there was any truth to the claim, it was a powerful one. Americans felt that Communists were trying to take this crucial choice—along with many others—away from them. This provoked a fear that easily developed into hatred.

Likewise, ethnicity and religion can also be used to divide people. By convincing members of one group that they are in direct competition with another group, the propagandist may create an "us vs. them" scenario.

"The suspicion under which the Jews are held is murder. They are charged with enticing Gentile children and Gentile adults, butchering them, and draining their blood. They are charged with mixing this blood into their mass's unleavened bread and using it to practice superstitious magic…" —From *Der Sturmer*, the Nazi Party's newspaper, 1934

From the perspective of the propagandist, this division creates many opportunities—these negative emotions can be channeled to produce whatever effect is desired. Such scenarios are very harmful to the public, which is now governed by hatred, rather than reason. When you're faced with propaganda that seems to encourage hatred of a particular group, try to distance yourself from it emotionally. Identify where your hatred comes from and ask yourself whether it is truly justified, or whether it may have been fostered by propaganda.

Xenophobia is a specific kind of hatred and distrust directed against foreigners. Encouraging xenophobia is one of the easiest methods a propagandist can use to rouse people to action, particularly in countries with a strong sense of nationalism. Like many other forms of hate, xenophobia builds on the fear that one group is undermining another group's success. Rather than giving foreigners the benefit of the doubt and rationally considering the benefits they may offer a society, xenophobic people instead assume that the very presence of "outsiders" is a threat.

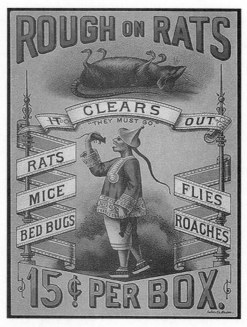

This advertisement for a pest killer takes advantage of xenophobic sentiments toward Chinese immigrants. Like many nations around the world, the United States has a history of xenophobic propaganda. This image depicts a Chinese man, with a braid that resembles a rat's tail, eating rodents. The slogan "They Must Go," seems to be applied not only to the vermin, but also to the Chinese population.

Thankfully, xenophobia has become less acceptable in large segments of society. This doesn't mean it has disappeared, however. Should you ever find that you're expected to take a certain course of action based only on a dislike of a given ethnic group, ask yourself whether there is really any logic behind the message. Often, xenophobic propaganda is entirely hollow except for its appeal against foreigners, and, if this is the case, feel free to reject it entirely—and take future arguments from that individual with a particularly large dose of skepticism.

Many negative emotions are closely related. Fear can grow into anger, and anger can develop into hatred and distrust.

CHAPTER 21: PROMOTING DISCRIMINATION, VIOLENCE, AND PROPERTY VIOLATION

Now that we have discussed some of the negative feelings propagandists can inspire, we are ready to look at some of the ways these feelings can be put to use. Unfortunately, there is almost no limit to the amount of destruction that can be wrought by fear, anger, hatred, and distrust. To begin, we'll look at some of the more common negative actions inspired by propaganda: discrimination, violence, and property violation.

DISCRIMINATION

Discrimination is unfair treatment based on prejudice. Closely related to xenophobia and racism, it commonly occurs along ethnic and national lines. However, people also discriminate on the basis of religion, gender, age, physical appearance, weight, or any number of other factors. Discrimination is a seemingly constant blight in our world and a constant source of conflict.

It may be difficult to understand why anyone would try to promote discrimination; it is clearly harmful and unethical. Nevertheless, discrimination can serve many different purposes. Thus, a surprising amount of propaganda is devoted to encouraging discrimination.

"We began by saying that a cockroach cannot give birth to a butterfly. It is true. A cockroach gives birth to another cockroach.... The history of Rwanda shows us clearly that a Tutsi stays always exactly the same..."—from an extremist newspaper in Rwanda in 1993, published by the Hutu faction, to incite radical discrimination and violence against the Tutsis

There are two main reasons one group might try to encourage discrimination against another group. Being able to recognize these motives can help you to analyze the propaganda you may be faced with. One possible reason for promoting discrimination is ideological: people may want to promote discrimination simply because of their own hatred, and they may actually believe that discrimination is morally sound. The second possible motivation is strategic: people may find that it serves their interests to promote discrimination or to pit two groups against one another.

Ideological propaganda is commonly seen from hate groups. The Ku Klux Klan, for example, has, at various times, issued very strong propaganda against African Americans and other groups. However, ideological campaigns need not be as obvious as those used by the KKK. Eugenicists, for example, may use very subtle propaganda to promote a population decrease among ethnic minorities or the disabled. This type of propaganda, however subtle in design, is classified as ideological because it attempts to promote the propagandist's beliefs.

"We should hire three or four colored ministers... with engaging personalities. The most successful educational approach to the Negro is through a religious appeal. We do not want the word to go out that we want to exterminate the Negro population. And the minister is the man who can straighten out that idea if it ever occurs to any of their more rebellious members." —a letter from Planned Parenthood founder, Margaret Sanger, to a fellow eugenicist

Purely strategic discrimination, on the other hand, is even more calculated; it promotes discrimination on an entirely self-serving basis. Propagandists who promote discrimination for purely strategic purposes may or may not believe that what they are doing is morally sound—they simply promote it as a way of achieving their own objectives. Propaganda of this kind often comes from governments, corporations, or political factions.

During World War II, for example, the US government issued a great deal of propaganda stigmatizing the Japanese. While the messages usually spoke against the people living in Japan, they had the added effect of promoting discrimination against Japanese Americans. Later, this made it much easier for the government to gather Japanese Americans in internment camps without raising objections from their fellow Americans.

This kind of vilification of the Japanese was common in World War II propaganda.

Although such racist uses of propaganda are regrettable, there are, remarkably, discrimination-based campaigns that many would consider benevolent. For instance, consider anti-smoking propaganda in the United States. While the main intent of these campaigns might be to stigmatize the act of smoking, many stigmatize smokers themselves. Strategically, this makes a great deal of sense. If one of the main contributors to youth smoking is peer pressure, then promoting discrimination against smokers would seem to be the ideal countermeasure. Likewise, the overweight are often targets of negative press in diet advertisements and in the news media. While the attention to obesity is intended to warn people of health risks associated with excess weight, these portrayals help to stigmatize the overweight.

Regardless of whether you think that promoting discrimination is ever justified, it is important to be able to recognize when such propaganda is aimed at you, so that you can make rational, informed decisions. If a poster, or speech, or commercial makes sweeping generalizations about members of a given group, you may want to look at it more critically.

VIOLENCE

There are not many situations in which violence is deemed appropriate and socially acceptable; cases of war and self-defense are among the few scenarios in which acts of violence are generally considered justifiable. For this reason, propaganda that openly promotes violence is relatively rare. Aggression can be easily provoked in people who have been conditioned to feel fear, anger, hatred, or distrust. Hence, propaganda that appeals to these sentiments often lays the groundwork for an outright call to violence. If discord has been fueled by propaganda, it may not take much work to transform tension into aggression.

The poster above encourages violence toward Chinese Americans. According to the sketch, Americans should strike out at the Chinese. Note the contrast between the detailed, realistic face of the Caucasian man and the cartoonish, almost subhuman, image of the Asian man.

Violence can serve a number of purposes a government might find useful. It might, for instance, pave the way for further violent action by a government. A nation like Nazi Germany may begin by inciting violence against the targeted group. Then, once people are accustomed to that violence, they may be less likely to oppose forced deportations or mass executions.

The caption of this World War I poster reads simply, "Serbia must die!"

In a similar technique, inciting violence may serve as a distraction from a completely unrelated government agenda. For example, if a government wishes to eliminate its nation's health care system, it might encounter public opposition. However, if the government first institutes a system of propaganda that provokes violence, such policy changes may go unnoticed. If people are occupied with defending themselves from immediate violence, they will have much less energy to devote to fighting government reforms.

In some cases, violence itself may be the desired end. For example, a radical anarchist group might incite aggression as a way of directly battling the government. A hate group might encourage hostility as a way of chasing away or killing the group they hate. Settlers might use force to displace the people whose land they are trying to settle. Propaganda that promotes violence is useful in a wide range of circumstances. However, it is also easy to spot; as long as you guard your emotions, it is unlikely that you'll be deceived by this style of propaganda.

PROPERTY VIOLATION

In the modern world, there is not much propaganda devoted to encouraging widespread theft. Historically, however, propaganda promoting property violation was not so exceptional. Most often, theft is promoted in conjunction with discrimination. It may be wrong to steal, but, once people have been stripped of their dignity and humanity, it is relatively easy to rob them of their material possessions as well. Such campaigns are most easily executed against an ethnic or religious minority. A government is usually involved, often playing a primary role. Land, businesses, and assets may all be considered fair game if they belong to the targeted group. The confiscation of personal property may be facilitated by the government through legal means, or, just as commonly, it may simply be the state's policy to ignore such theft. Hence, a member of the majority group may settle on land owned by a member of the minority group, bringing about the displacement and ultimate removal of the minority. Promoting theft is often part of a broader campaign to get rid of a group entirely. It may precede a movement of violence, or, the group whose property and rights are constantly at risk may find it easier to simply move to another area.

"And there where Serbian blood is shed and Serbian bones fall must be Serbian land. Those who think otherwise are on the side of our enemy… "—from the Serbian publication Borba

The agenda to eliminate an entire segment of the population is rarely stated openly. More often, it is framed in positive terms, either ignoring the original owners entirely or making it seem that they are not entitled to their property. A campaign might, for example, seem to tell people to go settle an 'unsettled' area, or an area that is not being used to its full potential. Stealing another person's property would be described as a duty to properly utilize resources. Consider, for instance, the term "Manifest Destiny," which was used to promote American settlement of the entire North American continent. In a powerful example of assertion, this phrase suggested that it was the obvious, divine right of European Americans to dominate the continent and subjugate its original inhabitants, the Native Americans.

This 1872 painting by John Gast, entitled, "American Progress" illustrates the idea of Manifest Destiny: that westward expansion was the obvious, divinely ordained fate of the United States.

Another technique often employed to disenfranchise unpopular groups is to portray them as immoral. By indicating that they came into possession of their property through illegal means, or that their way of life is inferior, the propagandist may put their rights of ownership into question. In virtually all such propaganda, there is an ostensible reason to divest people of their property, however illogical.

> Once a propagandist has inspired fear, anger, and hatred,
> the road has been paved for discrimination, violence, and
> property violation of a perceived "enemy."

CHAPTER 22: DEHUMANIZATION AND THE VIOLATION OF HUMAN RIGHTS

When we talked about inciting anger, hatred, or violence, we touched briefly on dehumanization. In this technique, a propagandist will portray a particular group of people as being less than human, not deserving of human rights. By dehumanizing people, a propagandist can create apathy toward injustices committed against them. In this chapter, we will elaborate on the reprehensible, but powerful uses of dehumanizing propaganda.

Dehumanization can play a very important role in creating a sense of indifference. The propagandist may not ask people to commit any acts of brutality themselves, but merely to passively accept the atrocities committed around them. If people feel sympathetic toward the maligned group, they may protest—especially in democratic settings. But, if they already feel that the targeted group is somehow inferior, they will be much less likely to invest their time and energy in complaining.

In the 1940 Nazi propaganda film, The Eternal Jew (Der Ewige Jude), the Jewish people are likened to rats, overrunning Germany.

One of the most effective ways to encourage apathy is to foster a sense of difference between two groups. The propagandist may begin by exaggerating the differences between one group and another.

This image attempts to establish a significant difference between the English, represented by Florence Nightingale, and the Irish, as represented by the fictitious figure, "Bridget McBruiser." The Irish, like many immigrant groups, were falsely stereotyped as less evolved and less civilized than their Anglo-American counterparts.

Above, we see two examples of how evolutionary theory was used to promote the idea that some ethnic groups are less evolved—less human than others. Here, the Irish are compared to chimpanzees and dogs, and these claims are supported by absurdly unrealistic drawings.

Once a real or imaginary difference has been established, it can be surprisingly easy to dehumanize people. It is a simple technique that transforms a sense of "otherness" into a complete disregard for a group's well-being. Nevertheless, we can see the same basic tactics being used to justify atrocities throughout history.

In most modern contexts, dehumanizing, apathy-inducing propaganda is more subtle, but no less dangerous. It is rare to see an overt call to violence, but propaganda that directs us to look the other way or slowly erodes the humanity of a given group is always out there and can be difficult to recognize.

"Every Hutu must know that the Tutsi woman, wherever she may be, is working for the Tutsi ethnic cause. In consequence, any Hutu is a traitor who: Acquires a Tutsi wife; Acquires a Tutsi concubine; Acquires a Tutsi secretary or protégée....Hutu must stop taking pity on the Tutsi... " – From The Hutu Ten Commandments, published in Kangura in 1990, preceding the Rwandan genocide.

Dehumanizing a group of people can be a very effective way of justifying a war effort. In modern warfare, it is common for hundreds, or even thousands of civilians to be killed and considered "collateral damage" in a time of war. This can be a serious problem for the nation waging war, from a public relations standpoint. If the loss of twenty soldiers can provoke a crisis of conscience for people, it is equally probable that the loss of a hundred innocent civilians could provoke unrest. An example can be found in the My Lai massacre, which took place during the Vietnam War. In this incident, hundreds of Vietnamese civilians were murdered. When news of the massacre made its way to the American public, the anti-war movement grew rapidly.

One way in which a government at war can try to minimize the negative impact of civilian casualties is to dehumanize the civilian population. If people think of the population as less than human, or at least less worthy of life than their own soldiers, it is easier to gain support for the war effort. The enemy population may be depicted as violent, unintelligent, or "primitive." Being at war naturally creates this sort of "us vs. them" mentality, but propaganda can be used to reinforce it and to steer it in a particular direction.

This Dr. Seuss propaganda cartoon from World War II is an example of dehumanizing wartime propaganda. During the war, a myth circulated in the United States that Japanese Americans constituted a "5th Column" of the Japanese army. This cartoon shows the Japanese on the West Coast lining up to collect explosives. By depicting the Japanese as almost identical drones, happily following orders, the cartoon makes them seem somewhat less than human. Propaganda like this laid the groundwork for the later incarceration of innocent Japanese Americans in detention camps.

A great deal of propaganda during World War II played on the widespread racism of the era. Germans and Italians were figures of caricature, but none were so viciously attacked as the Japanese. Asian immigrants had long been victims of racism in America. After the bombing of Pearl Harbor and America's entry into the Pacific theatre, however, this undercurrent swelled to the surface. Caricatures of the Japanese could be seen in newspapers, comic books, movies, and especially in propaganda posters. It is important to realize just how powerful such hate-filled propaganda can be—even when promoting causes we might otherwise agree with.

World War II propaganda often depicted the Japanese as having fangs, pointed ears, and other distorted features.

As we've already discussed, prejudice can be very destructive. Taken to an extreme, it can even end in genocide: a systematic movement to eradicate an entire group of people. The key element in promoting genocide is dehumanization. Propaganda is used to present the idea that there is a fundamental difference between people—some deserve to live, and others do not. Shades of grey cannot be admitted if a genocidal movement is to be effective. There must be simple criteria to determine the difference between a person deserving of human rights and a member of the "subhuman" group.

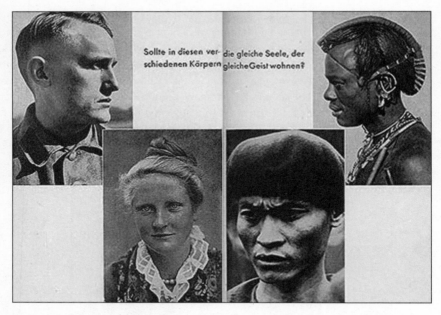

Sollte in diesen verschiedenen Körpern die gleiche Seele, der gleiche Geist wohnen?

From an SS pamphlet outlining Nazi theories of race and evolution, these images are accompanied by the question, "Does the same soul, the same living spirit dwell in these differing bodies?" Here, the humanity of non-Germans is openly called into question.

Setting up such criteria can have the added effect of provoking fear in a great portion of the population, since many people will find themselves in a grey area somewhere between one group and the other. In a bid to prove they belong to the majority group, these people will often become the most ardent zealots for the cause of genocide.

When paving the way for genocide, it is vital for propagandists to inspire hatred while eliminating the humanity of the target group.

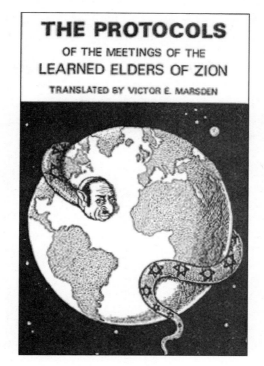

This image is from the cover of The Protocols of the Elders of Zion, one of the most widely disseminated propagandistic forgeries ever made. The text delineates a fictitious plan by the Jewish people to dominate the world. Many different anti-Semitic groups, including the Nazis, have used this forgery to garner support for their campaigns of genocide.

Folk legends regarding the evils of a group are very effective in promoting the necessary level of fear. Detailed conspiracies about wide-ranging plots are also useful.

"The Armenians are in league with the enemy. They will launch an uprising in Istanbul, kill off the Ittihadist leaders and will succeed in opening the straits [of the Dardanelles]." —Ottoman propaganda from 1914

Although hate groups such as the KKK might promote genocidal goals, they are, thankfully, unable to achieve them. However, when a government is involved, as in Nazi Germany, genocide can become a hideous reality.

"Now there is war! The Jews forced us into a struggle for life and death….The devilish hatred of the Jews plunged the world into war, need and misery. Our holy hate will bring us victory and save all of mankind."–from an editorial published by a Nazi newspaper during World War II

Many of the uses of dehumanizing propaganda are dangerous and destructive, but genocide is arguably the worst. Unfortunately, genocidal propaganda continues to play a role in the world today, and it all begins with dehumanization. Whenever you're presented with the idea that some people's lives are inherently less valuable than others, for whatever reason, it is quite possible that you are looking at an instance of dehumanizing, and potentially deadly, propaganda.

After a group has been dehumanized in the eyes of the community, there is nothing to protect them from human rights abuses, including genocide.

CHAPTER 23: DEIFICATION

It takes an extreme propaganda campaign to fully dehumanize a group. It takes nearly as intense an effort, however, to raise a group or an individual far above everyone else. Nevertheless, clever propaganda can make even the most ordinary human being seem like a god.

The figures that are deified are often at the center of a pivotal social movement, or are important leaders of a country. In totalitarian nations, the leader is nearly always deified—indeed, a great deal of the state's propaganda efforts may be geared toward that purpose—in order to further cement the power of the state.

In the most obvious examples of deification, an individual may literally be viewed as a god by his or her followers. This can be accomplished by propaganda that promises people a greater purpose in life. Miracles and evidence of the divine will be fabricated or simply exaggerated to lend credibility to the person's divinity.

In the 1990s, the Reverend Sun Myung Moon declared that he was the Messiah, and that he and his wife were the True Parents of humanity.

"Ladies and Gentlemen, what is the Messiah? The Messiah is the True Parents of humankind. God's original plan was to establish perfected Adam and Eve as the true ancestors of humanity. Satan, however, invaded this ideal, and God, ever since, has been working toward the emergence of ideal True Parents through which all humankind can be restored. As True Fathers and True Mothers ourselves, we must vanquish Satan, liberate humanity, and build the kingdom of Heaven on earth."

This style of propaganda is not common, in its most obvious forms, but it can still be found throughout the world. Various cults have been formed by individuals claiming some form of divinity, often using this status as justification for controversial actions.

In this German poster from the 1930s, Adolf Hitler is deified through dramatic imagery. The glowing light creates the effect of a halo, calling to mind traditional depictions of Christ and the saints. The image of the descending eagle is reminiscent of the dove descending on Jesus at his baptism. Even Hitler's position in the foreground, elevated above the troops, serves to make him appear much more important than the ordinary man.

More commonly, however, propaganda will not claim literal divinity for a leader, but merely an extremely elevated position. This kind of deification is often just as powerful. By claiming some sort of divine mandate or supernatural wisdom, political leaders can justify almost any action. No longer needing to depend on endorsements from others, they are able to make their own policy with impunity.

And because they are ascribed powers of reasoning beyond those of the rest of us, their logic is beyond question. This is perhaps one of the most dangerous forms of propaganda, simply because it removes the potential that there will be an easy avenue to rational discourse in the future. Once deification has taken place, logic is entirely excluded from the picture.

Mao Zedong was very skilled in the use of deification propaganda. As the Communist Revolution in China progressed, propaganda using Mao's likeness became more and more refined. The images were painted in bright shades, creating a sense of warmth and light. The color red, signifying good fortune to the Chinese, was featured prominently in each painting. Over time, the disembodied head of Mao, hovering above the jubilant people, became iconic. In this image, Mao is literally portrayed as the shining sun, a truly godlike figure.

In troubled times, people may actually welcome the deification of a leader. It can be comforting to feel that a divinely powerful person is in control.

This illustration of President Roosevelt is typical of presidential propaganda during WWII. While not as extreme as the images of Mao and Hitler, this picture does, nevertheless, present the president as a godlike figure. The clouds in the background and the flood of light create a heavenly effect, and the billowing American flag links Roosevelt directly with the United States itself.

Outside of the government arena, leaders of organizations and movements are also occasionally deified. Once elevated to a godlike status, they hold even greater sway, and are much less open to questioning or debate. This provides a movement with a central, guiding voice and removes internal dissent and fracture. The short-term benefits of cohesion may be seen as a worthwhile trade-off for the freedom and equality that are sacrificed.

In many cases, deification of an individual takes place after he or she is dead. Indeed, this can be a much easier task for the propagandist than deifying a living person. Public opinion is generally forgiving toward the dead, and opposition to the propagandist's aims can be looked upon as unkind and insensitive.

"Oh Englishman, the god Gandhiji came in the end and your days have been numbered." –During the late Colonial era in India, there was a great deal of propaganda deifying Gandhi. Stories of his divine powers were spread, and some castes were told that he was a new god, sent by Siliya and Simaliya to look after them.

Sometimes, the aggrandizement of a given person may have positive effects. For example, Gandhi's glorification may have led some to heed his message of non-violence and equality. Nevertheless, while it may seem rather harmless at first, it can be argued that deification is actually one of the most dangerous uses of propaganda discussed in this book. Just as dehumanization can lead to great atrocities, the deification technique has been used to justify everything from the 1978 Jonestown Massacre to the Holocaust.

Once a leader has been deified in the eyes of followers, there is no limit to his or her power.

CONCLUSION

In the preceding pages, we've looked at many different techniques of propaganda, from ads aimed at selling dog food to slogans that have inspired genocides. We've seen propaganda used by all kinds of people: the kind and the cruel, dictators and underdogs, the sophisticated and the simple. It has been used to inspire and condone the most evil actions imaginable. But, at other times, propaganda has been used to promote kindness, generosity, and courage.

In each of these instances, there has been one uniting thread: no matter what the purpose, what the scope, what the medium, all of the techniques of propaganda we've discussed have undermined the importance of sound logic. This is the fundamental characteristic that sets propaganda apart from other forms of communication. Decisions should be made through careful thought and deliberation. They should be made after hearing all of the facts from all sides of a debate, with sufficient opportunity for discourse and a chance to weigh all of the benefits and costs. But propaganda encourages us to bypass all of these considerations.

Like many things in life, propaganda itself is not intrinsically "good" or "evil." Ultimately, only you can decide where to draw the line between acceptable and offensive propaganda. But, as you've seen in this book, distinguishing between reason and emotion is an important first step toward making that decision.

The ability to distinguish the emotional appeals of propaganda from sound argumentation frees us to make informed choices. No one would deny that emotions and instincts are essential to the human experience; in relationships, in entertainment, and in art, emotion adds meaning to our lives. But the problem arises when emotion is allowed to override reason. The trouble is that our emotions are sometimes controlled by outsiders who do not have our best interests in mind.

The conclusions we draw through reason may not always be "true" or "right." Nevertheless, engaging in logical thought has a number of benefits. For one, we are able to explain to others how we arrived at a given conclusion. They may find our reasoning convincing and be swayed, or they may see flaws in our logic and reveal those flaws to us. This provides another benefit: the ability to change our conclusions in light of new evidence. When reason guides us, our conclusions are not static; our perspectives can grow and evolve.

Over the course of this book, much of the propaganda we've presented has come from television and print media—one-sided sources of information that don't invite inquiry or debate. As you think about the messages that bombard you from day to day, remember to question the motives behind them and the logic employed. Ask yourself if you are seeing both sides of the issue. Is each perspective represented with equal accuracy and force? Are the important questions being asked? If not, is there a way for you to ask those questions yourself? A lively forum for discussion is your most effective defense against propaganda. Always be on the lookout for dissenting opinions—even if you have to search to find them. In this modern age of ready information, it is possible to find almost every side of every issue, and it is a worthwhile investment to make.

When we take responsibility for what we believe and how we behave, we never have to say that we were tricked, manipulated, or caught up in a wave of passion. We can explain the mistakes we've made and defend the actions we've taken if they are based on logic and not merely emotions. By practicing independent thinking, we commit ourselves to behaving as responsible, free agents in a world dominated by propaganda.

CUMULATIVE EXERCISES

ACTIVITY 1

Directions: Fill in the blanks with the name of a propaganda technique that is used in the previous sentence. Answers may be used more than once.

Moderator: Ladies and gentlemen, we are proud to live in the greatest country the world has ever known. _____ And, as we all know, the ability to voice differing opinions is what has made the United States what it is today. _____ So, let me welcome you to the presidential debate, where we will hear from Governor Tyson of Ohio and Senator Grummann of Tennessee.

Tyson: Thank you for your generous applause. It is a great honor for me, the daughter of a coal miner, _____ to stand before you and discuss some of the most important issues of our time, the issues that will determine if we develop solutions to our current problems or find ourselves enslaved to foreign powers. _____

My misguided opponentv_____ would have you believe that his plans will preserve national security, but the vast majority of Americans favor my proposal _____ to annex various U.S. territories, providing this great nation with the stability and strength we need to remain the world's leading superpower. _____

Grummann: I have no doubt that Ms. Tyson has the best intentions, but her plan is naive. _____ The president of the American Institute for Foreign Policies _____ has stated, "Annexing territories like Puerto Rico, Guam, and the Virgin Islands and making them states will diminish our national identity and threaten our security." _____ And I say to you that I agree with him: If we give these people the rights of American citizens, they will decrease our standard of living, they will make each one of our votes worth less, and their linguistic and cultural differences will soon destroy our culture.

_____

Tyson: On the contrary, Mr. Grummann: The USA will soon be destroyed by forces beyond its control if we do not implement these changes immediately. I will admit that my plan is not ideal, but it is better than the alternative of leaving our territories open to invasion. _____ Left to fend for themselves, these territories will provide offshore havens for terrorists. _____
We need to treat this ongoing problem with the seriousness that we applied to the Manhattan Project, which helped defeat the Japanese in World War II, with the strength of Ronald Reagan, when he demanded the destruction of the Berlin Wall, and with the foresight of JFK, as he focused our sights on the space race.

_____

Grummann: This kind of rhetoric from Washington insiders like Ms. Tyson is the source of our nation's current problems. _____ There is no connection between the historic issues Ms. Tyson has mentioned and our present dilemma. _____

There are only two options for the American public: you either stand with me and agree that the United States has a need for security that goes beyond our borders, or you agree with my opponent that our only hope of safety lies in bringing every country in the world under our protection. _____ We could have settled this divisive issue years ago, but legislators of Ms. Tyson's party, whose motives were less than patriotic, _____ decided to postpone making this decision until they left office. _____

Tyson: Allow me to point out that in the years since Senator Grummann's party has had control of Congress, the issue still has not been resolved. _____ However, I am not here to dole out blame, but to offer a solution. And statistics prove that extending a hand to those less fortunate and adopting a policy of inclusion always helps America. _____ I am confident that, once I am president, the entire country will join my supporters in seeing the value of my plan. _____

ACTIVITY 2

For each of the images on pages 152-155, answer the following questions:

A. Identify a possible audience and purpose for this poster.

B. Is this an example of propaganda? Why, or why not?

C. Identify which, if any of the techniques of propaganda discussed in the book, are being used in the image, and explain how. (Each image may include more than one technique.)

D. Does this image appeal to emotions? Which emotions are targeted?

E. Does the poster include an example of faulty reasoning? If so, identify the flawed argument and explain why it is illogical.

1.

A.

B.

C.

D.

E.

2.

A.

B.

C.

D.

E.

3.

A.

B.

C.

D.

E.

4.

A.

B.

C.

D.

E.

ACTIVITY 3

Create an original propaganda campaign based on one of the following scenarios:

1. Imagine that you are an advertiser, promoting a product. Using at least five of the eleven techniques of propaganda described in this book, create a campaign that will sell your fictitious brand.

2. Imagine that you are a politician who is running for office. Using at least five of the eleven techniques of propaganda described in this book, create a campaign that will get you elected.

3. Imagine that you are a social activist, promoting a cause. Using at least five of the eleven techniques of propaganda described in this book, create a campaign that will inspire people to join your cause.

A successful campaign will make use of a variety of media, such as:

- posters
- leaflets
- slogans
- essays
- speeches
- debates
- film presentations

Keep in mind that, in order to qualify as propaganda, your campaigns must have each of the following:

- persuasive function
- sizeable target audience
- representation of a specific group's agenda
- use of faulty reasoning and/or emotional appeals